Better Homes and Gardens®

step-by-step

shade gardens

Patricia A. Taylor

Better Homes and Gardens® Books
Des Moines, Iowa

Better Homes and Gardens® Books
An imprint of Meredith® Books

Step-by-Step Shade Gardens
Senior Editor: Marsha Jahns
Production Manager: Douglas Johnston

Vice President and Editorial Director: Elizabeth P. Rice
Executive Editor: Kay Sanders
Art Director: Ernest Shelton
Managing Editor: Christopher Cavanaugh

President, Book Group: Joseph J. Ward
Vice President, Retail Marketing: Jamie L. Martin
Vice President, Direct Marketing: Timothy Jarrell

Meredith Corporation
Chairman of the Executive Committee: E. T. Meredith III
Chairman of the Board and Chief Executive Officer:
    Jack D. Rehm
President and Chief Operating Officer: William T. Kerr

Produced by ROUNDTABLE PRESS, INC.
Directors: Susan E. Meyer, Marsha Melnick
Executive Editor: Amy T. Jonak
Editorial Director: Anne Halpin
Senior Editor: Jane Mintzer Hoffman
Design: Brian Sisco, Susan Evans, Sisco & Evans, New York
Photo Editor: Marisa Bulzone
Assistant Editor: Alexis Wilson
Assistant Photo Editor: Carol Sattler
Encyclopedia Editor: Henry W. Art and Storey
    Communications, Inc., Pownal, Vermont
Horticultural Consultant: Christine M. Douglas
Copy Editor: Sue Heinemann
Proofreader: Cathy Peck
Step-by-Step Photography: Derek Fell
Garden Plans: Elayne Sears and Storey Communications, Inc.

All of us at Meredith® Books are dedicated to providing you
with the information and ideas you need for successful
gardening. We guarantee your satisfaction with this book for
as long as you own it. If you have any questions, comments,
or suggestions, please write to us at:

Meredith® Books, *Garden Books*
Editorial Department, RW206
1716 Locust St.
Des Moines, IA 50309–3023

STEP-BY-STEP

Shade Gardens

The Qualities of Shade

*t*he greening of America—the maturing of trees and shrubs planted 20 or 30 years ago on bare suburban lots—is in full force. With the growth of these woody plants and the construction of buildings in urban areas, shade has made its mark on the American landscape. • But lack of sun does not mean you cannot grow plants. This book shows how to design and construct gardens filled with hundreds of beautiful plants that grow well in varying kinds of shade. • Bulbs, annuals, ground covers, perennials, shrubs, and trees suitable for shade are all covered in this volume. Although the choice of plants and designs for shade gardens can be daunting, the pleasure you'll get in the lovely shade garden setting that you create is well worth the effort.

Hot-Colored Shade Plants

Although shade flowers generally fall in the pastel ranges, several plants bear in hot colors, such as red, yellow, or orange blossoms. For example, you'll find bright reds on hardy fuchsia (F. magellanica), impatiens, cardinal flower (Lobelia cardinalis), and beebalm (Monarda didyma). Tuberous begonia, Turk's-cap lily (L. superbum), and flame azalea (Rhododendron calendulaceum) all feature fiery orange flowers. To add a burst of yellow flowers to your garden, plant lady's-mantle (Alchemilla vulgaris), Siberian pea tree (Caragana arborescens), golden star (Chrysogonum virginianum), or moneywort (Lysimachia nummularia).

*T*he first plantings that we now describe as ornamental gardens were created as shaded retreats about 2,500 years ago in the inner courtyards of the homes of wealthy Persians. These enclosed areas offered a cool, serene setting, an escape from the heat and turmoil outside.

Trees and buildings provided the sources of shade in these gardens. The gardens received lots of light, however, from the bright, light colored, and reflective walls around them. In addition, the courtyards incorporated carefully constructed geometric waterways that not only irrigated the plantings but also let beams of light bounce from the glassy water surface into darkened areas.

The popularity of ornamental gardens eventually spread to Mediterranean lands, where these sanctuaries were placed in spots bathed by sun—a hallmark of the region's climate. With the move into the sun, however, the idea of a garden as a cool retreat was discarded. Gardens became places of flowering color, sometimes riotous and sometimes subdued. It is really quite remarkable that throughout the history of Western gardens, there has been a consistent emphasis on creating gardens in sun.

Although there were always some shaded settings for people to enjoy in summer, particularly on large estates, these were not the garden areas. With the growth of home ownership associated with the rise of the middle class, however, the average property size of homesteads began to shrink dramatically. The great estates of the past contained thousands of acres; today, a plot of two to five acres is considered a large amount of property. Indeed, even a one-acre yard

seems a vast tract, especially to city dwellers gardening in tiny lots or in containers lined up on windowsills and fire escapes.

No matter what the size of the growing area, however, the false idea has persisted that you cannot have colorful flowers in shady settings. Only a few shade plants have been grown over the years. Some enterprising souls planted snowdrops *(Galanthus* spp.*)* and winter aconites *(Eranthis hyemalis),* two bulbs that flower in early spring sunlight, before trees overhead leaf out. Some gardeners added spring-flowering shrubs, such as rhododendrons and mountain laurels *(Kalmia latifolia),* to their properties. Otherwise, until the recent advent of mass-produced colorful impatiens, shade settings remained expanses of dark green.

One of the reasons impatiens rank among the most popular bedding plants today is because there is so much shade in American yards. Impatiens are durable, easy to grow, and bloom all summer. For the past several decades, people have flocked to these annual flowers to add color to their surroundings. But once they planted impatiens, most gardeners stopped, not knowing where to look for other plants that would perform successfully in shady conditions. This book seeks to expand the horizons of shade gardeners by describing how to design and care for gardens with hundreds of gorgeous plants that flourish in the shade, including many plants that will not thrive in sunny settings. Shade can be an asset rather than a liability for gardeners who know how to work with it.

Before exploring the beauties of shade gardening, let's take a look at the benefits of shade, as well as the different types of shade.

Many plants will thrive in a location that receives dappled shade for most of the day. In the foreground is a native fringe tree (Chionanthus virginicus).

Plants for Heavy Shade

Even the darkest areas of the garden are suitable for a variety of shade plants. If you're looking for shrubs, choose fatsia (F. japonica), sweet box (Sarcococca hookerana var. humilis), or skimmia (S. japonica). The many shade-tolerant ground covers include carpet bugleweed (Ajuga reptans), wild ginger (Asarum spp.), Kenilworth ivy (Cymbalaria muralis), and pachysandra. Wall fern (Polypodium vulgare), annual impatiens, perennial bear's-breech (Acanthus mollis), and baneberry (Actaea spp.) are also excellent candidates for areas with fairly dense shade.

▼ **Benefits of Shade**

Remember that the gardens of ancient Persia were shaded retreats, oases of calm and serenity. You can think of shade gardens in much the same way today. After all, a shady garden is cooler than a sunny border in summer and is more pleasant to stroll through or to work in.

When properly designed and constructed, shade gardens are usually much easier to maintain than sunny ones. The soil doesn't dry out as fast in the shade, so you don't have to water as often. Weeds tend to grow more slowly. And there are fewer insect problems because such pests as aphids and caterpillars prefer sun.

In the southern part of the United States, shade is considered not only a benefit but often a downright necessity. Many plants that grow best in full sun in the North must be protected in the South, especially in the afternoon, as they cannot tolerate the burning light of the sun and the tremendous heat buildup that occurs throughout the day.

Finally, shade plants offer a wealth of foliage forms and textures that are not found among sun-loving plants. Hostas are a wonderful example of the sumptuous leaves of shade plants. The subtle delights of foliage can provide the basis of a garden. Indeed, many shade gardeners become so entranced by different foliage combinations—the gray-green and purple-tinged fronds of the Japanese painted fern *(Athyrium goeringianum* 'Pictum'*)* with the blue-green leaves of *Hosta sieboldiana* 'Elegans', for example—that they find it easy to create a garden of distinction and elegance without any flowers at all.

▼ **Types of Shade**

In this book any area that receives less than six hours of direct, unobstructed sun per day is considered shady. Shade, however, is an extremely broad term and, for gardening purposes, needs to be further defined. Here are some of the popular terms used to describe shade:

▼ *Light shade* is bright, open shade—the kind found at the edge of a woodland or on the north side of a white house. This is the type of shade that was prevalent in the Persian gardens of long ago. The high-canopied trees and bright walls buffered the garden area from intense heat while at the same time allowing light to suffuse the planting area. Careful plant choices will allow you to create a lovely garden with a diversity of form and color in a lightly shaded location.

▼ *Partial* or *half shade* describes a location that is in shade during part of the day, receiving from two to six hours of sun a day. If the shade is bright and open, you will find that most sun-loving plants can grow in this kind of situation.

▼ *Dappled shade* is the kind of shade created when trees filter sunlight. Plants are dotted with light in different patterns through the course of a day. If the garden receives dappled shade throughout the day, there should be enough sun to grow a wide variety of plants. Such a situation is sometimes considered partial shade. If the dapples are brief and the shade full for much of the day, you may want to make a few changes to let more light into the garden.

▼ *Heavy shade* is the solid kind of shade created by a large evergreen or a tall building. In the absence of any light reflectors, few plants can grow in deep shade if it is continuous throughout the day.

Flowering shrubs, such as the azaleas and rhododendrons adorned with delicate pink blossoms pictured here, are the glory of spring in the woodland shade garden.

▼ *Full shade* describes an area that receives no direct sun at all. Do not despair if this description fits your garden. Some plants can tolerate full shade, and there are also a number of ways you can modify the shade to let more light into the garden.

Be aware, too, that morning shade is different from afternoon shade. Afternoon shade can keep plants cooler on hot summer days and is especially advantageous for many plants in southern gardens, where summer heat is intense. Morning shade can sustain the cool of nighttime, so that when the hot afternoon sun finally does strike, the temperature change may shock the plants. It's best to locate the garden where it will receive afternoon rather than morning shade.

CHAPTER 1

Designing Gardens in the Shade

gardening in the refreshing coolness of shade enables you to work with a wealth of plants that feature voluptuous foliage as well as gorgeous flowers. • Because shade plants are subtler in color and texture than many of the bright-hued (in some cases even garish) sun lovers, you can reach a level of sophistication in your shade garden that is more difficult to achieve in a sunny garden. • When starting any garden, it is important to fully understand the setting before choosing the plants to fill it. This chapter starts with basic information on shaded environments, then provides guidelines on designing with flower color and foliage as well as with plant shapes and textures.

Understanding the Shaded Environment

TROUBLESHOOTING TIP

If you want a successful low-maintenance shade garden, plant only flowers and shrubs with light requirements that match the conditions in your growing area.

*E*very shaded environment—whether on a town plot or a country estate, at the seashore or in the mountains—is affected by four elements: the buildings or trees above; the ground below; the surrounding "walls," such as those created by hedges or fences; and the time of day or year. Given the many possible interrelationships among four elements, it is easy to see why defining and understanding your particular shaded environment are probably the most difficult tasks you will face in creating a shade garden.

▼ The View from Above

First consider the sources of shade. Look above your garden area to see what kind of tall structures are blocking the natural light. Are these obstacles artificial or natural? Is the shade these structures cast solid or dappled?

The shade cast by tall buildings, as city dwellers know only too well, is dense and solid and cannot be manipulated. This is unrelenting shade. All may not be lost, however. If the building is light-colored, it reflects light and creates what is known as bright shade. Also, if only the very tip of the building's shadow reaches your property, the condition is known as open (as opposed to closed) shade. Many plants will thrive in solid shade as long as it is bright and open.

If the shade in your garden area is due to trees, inspect them in early summer. At this time of year the trees have grown all their leaves, and you can see if the shade cast is dense (such as that under a maple) or dappled (such as that under a Japanese stewartia). Like the unrelenting shade formed by some buildings, dense shade cast by trees can make it almost impossible to create a garden. If the shade is dappled, however, enough sprinkled sunlight is available throughout the day for many plants to thrive.

▼ The Ground Below

Most shade plants evolved in woodland settings, which means they naturally grow in soil that is rich in organic matter from fallen leaves and branches that have decomposed. If you are installing a garden in an existing woodland, there is probably little that you will need to do to amend the soil to make it suitable for gardening.

If you are constructing a garden shaded by buildings, however, closely examine the soil. Amend it by adding leaf mulch, peat moss, and other organic materials to mimic the type of soil conditions that exist in the woods.

There are, however, areas in woodlands or under clumps of trees where the ground is relatively lifeless. The barren floor of a thick pine forest, for example, or the root-infested area around a large maple is a clear signal from nature that gardens are not meant to be constructed in such places. If such a location is all you have, take extra steps to amend the soil or, perhaps, build raised beds in the area.

▼ The Surrounding Walls

In addition to suffering in the shade caused by tall objects, many gardens are further darkened by such lower structures as shrubs or fences. Like trees and buildings, shrubs and fences can be solid or airy.

Walls, particularly those constructed of brick or dark stone, cast dense shadows but also absorb heat throughout the day and radiate it back into the air at night. Placing plants that love cool, shady conditions next to such constructions can be the equivalent of baking them in an oven.

When planted in masses, beautiful shrubs, such as rhododendrons and hydrangeas, may serve as walls around a garden area. Review the placement of

Shady areas of your property can be considerably brightened by painting nearby walls, including those of the house, to reflect light. Also try removing some of the limbs of trees to allow light to flood the ground level.

Understanding the Shaded Environment CONTINUED

1 Before planting a border of annuals, prepare the soil and examine the setting. Plants with white or red coloring would look handsome near this gray fence and birdbath.

2 Because this shady border is so narrow, there is no room for shrubs as a backdrop. The dramatic, colorful leaves of caladiums are perfect in such a situation.

3 Once the caladiums are in place, smaller plants can be grouped in front. The light pink flowers and red-tinged leaves of the begonia are a lovely complement.

4 To add interest, include other annuals with different forms and textures, such as these impatiens. Keep a consistent color theme so that the border doesn't look messy.

5 Once all your plants are in place, make sure the soil around each is firm. Water gently every day until the plants become established and fill the border.

Impatiens are among the easiest and most popular bedding plants in the country, decorating containers and borders from city settings to country estates. These low-maintenance plants simply require regular watering to brighten up any shady nook.

The large, strikingly colorful leaves of caladiums are beautiful additions to shade gardens. Use these plants in borders, as shown here, or in containers. Treated as annuals in all but tropical areas, these bulbs can be dug and stored over winter.

Understanding the Shaded Environment CONTINUED

Shade Bulbs for Early Spring Sun

Many bulbs burst into flower to greet the sun at the beginning of spring and then disappear in the coolness of shade throughout the remainder of the growing season. Consider planting pink corydalis (C. bulbosa), with its lovely pink flowers and gray-green foliage; winter aconite (Eranthis hyemalis), with its bright yellow blossoms; snowdrops (Galanthus nivalis), whose bright white flowers pop up through light snow covers; or Siberian squills (Scilla siberica), which form electric blue swaths of color in bare, late-winter settings.

shrubs carefully. If, however, the garden area is dark, you may want to move one or more shrubs to let in more light. To retain a feeling of enclosure, replace the denser shrubs with lighter, airier ones, such as white forsythia *(Abeliophyllum distichum)* or sweet pepperbush *(Clethra alnifolia)*. On the other hand, if there is already lots of light in an area you want for a shade garden, you can easily block some of it with evergreen rhododendrons or conifers.

▼ Seasonal Variations

The time of day or year is a crucial component in understanding the environment of your shade garden. Because the sun shifts its position in the sky slightly every day, causing the amount of light that falls on any given spot to change accordingly, the degree of shade is never constant.

In spring and fall, for example, the sun is lower in the sky. It no longer reaches over the buildings and evergreen trees that it scales with impunity in midsummer. Because the sun does not top these obstructions, long shadows are created. Areas that are sunny during summer are often shady in spring and fall.

On the other hand, in winter, when the sun is low in the sky, its rays reach under the lowest branches of evergreen trees and lighten areas that are normally quite dark. Make use of locations that get sun for only part of the year by growing seasonal plants that bloom or are at their best during the garden's brightest time.

Shade caused by deciduous trees changes dramatically with the seasons. Many late-winter and early-spring gardens consist of colorful plants that thrive when the sun streams through bare branches and are later protected from the summer heat by fully leafed-out trees.

1 *The first step in creating a ring garden around the base of a tree is to "scribe" the boundaries using string and a trowel. This method allows you to mark your planting area clearly.*

5 *It is a good idea to position plants above ground before you go through all the work of placing them in the soil. Check for height, color, and foliage contrasts.*

2 Once you are satisfied with the size of your proposed garden, clear the area. Work gently to avoid disturbing the tree roots, but be thorough removing all weeds.

3 After the ground is cleared, construct an edge for your garden. In this case, walnut logs act as a border. In other gardens, low stone walls form attractive boundaries.

4 Fill in the empty garden setting with good, loamy soil. Level the soil with a rake, and then let the soil settle for a day or two before you begin to plant.

6 Leave the arrangement in place while you plant each flower in its assigned position. Be sure each hole is wide enough to contain its plant's roots comfortably.

7 If you feel the planting area is too shady, thin overhead branches on the tree. Thinning can also make the tree itself healthier and more sculptural in appearance.

8 Water only after you are satisfied that your planting arrangement is just as you want it. Once the ground becomes wet and muddy, it is difficult to adjust plants.

Choosing the Best Site

Selecting a garden site is a very personal activity. The first step is to determine what you hope to achieve. Do you want a garden close by your front door, where you can see it as you come and go? Or do you want a secret garden tucked away in a woodland area? Perhaps you'd like a grand vista to view from various windows.

Another factor to consider is the density of the shade in your chosen spot. If the area has solid, dark shade that cannot be altered in any way, you will not be successful in creating a garden. Choose another spot where the shade is more manageable.

Some lucky shade gardeners have a property that offers several possible sites. If you belong to this group, pick a spot that is not mangled with tree roots and receives morning rather than afternoon sun.

▼ Shallow and Invasive Roots

Plants can be greedy. With certain trees—beeches (*Fagus* spp.) are particularly notorious—the roots do not burrow underground, so they gobble up all available nutrients and moisture at ground level, in many cases preventing other plants from growing nearby. While you can use containers and other gardening techniques, such as raised beds, to brighten the areas under such trees, it is a lot of work. It is better to choose another site, if possible.

Other trees have highly invasive roots, which spread readily underground and send up new tree shoots at will. These roots take away needed minerals and moisture from your plants, and the offshoot trees destroy the symmetry of your garden. Again, choose another site if possible. You should at least locate the garden beyond the trees' drip line to avoid the worst of the roots.

▼ The Heat Factor

The sun's intensity or warmth is a consideration in siting a garden, particularly in the southern states. Plants that grow well in shaded conditions are usually less heat tolerant than sun-loving plants. Indeed, in the South even plants that are sun lovers in the North must often be grown in afternoon shade.

Morning sun is fresh and cool; it hasn't had a chance to heat up the environment. By afternoon, however, the warmth of the sun is quite apparent. Many plants wilt under the heat buildup. This condition is exacerbated when the plants are near a light-reflecting object, such as white aluminum siding or bright patio stones. A bright surface can reflect heat—as well as light—into the garden.

Thus, if you live in the South, a particularly bad choice for a garden would be a west-facing site in front of a brick wall painted white. An excellent spot would be an area that receives morning sun and is east of a hedge, wall, or tall shrub.

▼ Other Features

After eliminating sites that are infested with tree roots or receive afternoon sun, look for places with built-in interest. Opt for an area with some variation in height (such as a sloping hillside), a few attractive trees, or perhaps a stone wall or other architectural feature.

Since shade gardens are cool retreats during the height of summer, you might consider whether a bench or gazebo can be installed in your chosen area.

Shaded by distant trees, the garden shown to the left is easy to plant because there are few, if any, competing tree roots in the garden bed.

Shallow-rooted plants, such as the perennial blue phlox (P. divaricata) and the biennial white money plant (Lunaria annua 'Alba'), are beautiful spring companions in a setting shaded by trees.

Types of Shade Gardens

Shade gardeners can choose from a variety of design options. The kind of garden you select is entirely up to you; there is no right or wrong choice. You can create a formal or informal setting, emphasize foliage or flowers, or design your garden with a mixed or singular plant scheme—while also ensuring that your garden is lovely throughout the year.

A formal garden has clearly defined borders and neatly executed plantings. Because there are so many elegant plants that thrive in the shade—regal rhododendrons, aristocratic astilbes, and choice caladiums, for example—it is very easy to construct a formal shade garden.

Charleston, South Carolina, is famous for its small, shady, formal courtyard gardens, bordered by looming homes and broken by red brick paths and lustrous black wrought-iron fences and gates. The tight, constricted nature of city life almost dictates a controlled, formal approach to gardening.

With an expansive space, such as a large wooded area, it is usually easiest to take an informal approach in constructing a shade garden. While its underlying structure must be as carefully thought out as that of a formal garden, the informal garden allows for more experimentation of plant combinations and a more easygoing arrangement. Instead of straight lines, the informal garden is full of curves.

Meandering paths, many with surprise gardens tucked in corners, are often a feature of informal gardens. Flowers are planted in flowing drifts of color. Ground covers are allowed to spread; for example, streams of blue phlox *(P. divaricata)* and splashes of creamy white foamflower *(Tiarella cordifolia)* are lovely in spring woods.

1 *To maximize flower and foliage color in a shade garden, use a mixture of plants. The setting shown above features annuals, perennials, and bulbs.*

Another design option is an all-foliage garden, which is both subtle and refreshing, particularly in the heat of midsummer. Hostas are especially striking foliage plants, bearing lush leaves in many sizes, textures, and hues (golds, blues, creamy whites, and rich greens). They also offer variegations featuring white, yellow, or chartreuse banded or speckled on different shades of green. Pair these bold plants with the lacy, delicate fronds of ferns to create stunning scenes.

While foliage gardens are attractive, they are not for everyone. Flowers are the true love of many gardeners, and fortunately there are hundreds of plants that need shade in order to bloom to their full potential. Widely available plants that contribute flowers for many weeks during the growing season include such annuals as impatiens and begonias, such perennials as celandine poppy *(Stylophorum diphyllum)* and

1 Instant borders can be created with potted caladiums. First, remove the caladium from its pot. If the roots are tightly wound, cut them apart before planting.

2 Using a garden trowel, as shown here, or a small spade, dig a hole that is large enough to comfortably contain the caladium, including its roots and potting soil.

3 Firm the soil in place after each caladium is in the ground. Once the entire row is planted, gently water the colorful display. This single-plant border requires little maintenance.

Creating a mixed border is the easiest way to ensure all-season color in a shade garden. This colorful garden features shrubs, perennial daylilies, and annual impatiens.

Types of Shade Gardens CONTINUED

yellow corydalis *(C. lutea)*, and such flowering shrubs as oakleaf hydrangea *(H. quercifolia)*. Using just these five plants—all described in the encyclopedia beginning on page 96—you can have a shade garden colored with flowers from spring through frost.

One popular shade garden design, the mixed border, combines all kinds of plants—shrubs, bulbs, annuals, and perennials—in a sumptuous composition. Shrubs are chosen for their flowers, their foliage, and their fall color. Bulbs are often placed where they will bloom in bare spots during late winter and early spring or add a dash of charm in late summer. Annuals supply color all summer with their continuous bloom. And perennials contribute both foliage and flowers to mixed borders.

Massed plantings, on the other hand, generally use only one or two specific plants to create their effects. Impatiens and begonias look quite dramatic when grouped in large numbers to form drifts of color or specific patterns. Other gardens feature just one kind of plant and concentrate a display within a specific period of time. Rhododendron or azalea gardens are particularly popular in this regard.

Without question, the shade garden is in its prime in spring. Hundreds of beautiful plants will bloom in the bright light under emerging tree buds and then go dormant or provide green foliage when the trees overhead become fully leafed out. Most rhododendrons and azaleas bloom in spring, as do forget-me-nots *(Myosotis scorpioides)*, green-and-gold *(Chrysogonum virginianum)*, trout lilies *(Erythronium spp.)*, Virginia bluebells *(Mertensia virginica)*, creeping phlox *(P. stolonifera)*, and many other beauties. You can take advantage of this bounty by designing a shade garden that is filled with color in spring

and then evolves into a cool, green retreat for the rest of the growing year.

Today, it is also easier to have multiseason color in the shade garden. The number of shade-loving plants readily available commercially has increased dramatically in recent years.

Tiny early spring and late summer bulbs are key components of a multiseason garden; they generally stay out of the way during summer and let other plants take top billing. Long-flowering shrubs, particularly those with some fall foliage color, such as oakleaf hydrangea *(H. quercifolia)* and sweet pepperbush *(Clethra alnifolia)*, are also important to an all-season border. Perennials and long-blooming annuals bear beautiful flowers from late spring through summer.

Whether in sun or shade, cacti are a prominent feature in desert gardens. These sculptural plants are particularly valued for their water-retaining capabilities.

The spare, elegant design and meticulously sculpted setting of this shady Pacific Coast garden reflect an oriental influence.

In San Francisco's Golden Gate Park, a shade garden offers stunning combinations of exotic semitropical tree ferns and beautiful native woodland plants.

Walled, shady courtyard gardens provide cool oases in such Southeastern cities as Charleston and Atlanta. Containers allow gardeners to display a variety of plants in the confined space.

Working with Color

Variegated Leaves

Choosing from the wealth of plants with variegated foliage is one of the pleasures of designing shade gardens. Popular shrubs with this attractive trait include the variegated lace-cap hydrangea (H. macrophylla 'Variegata'), which features large green leaves edged in white or cream; a special lily-of-the-valley bush (Pieris japonica 'Variegata'), whose dark green leaves have margins tinged in pink in spring, then fading to white; and a hardy fuchsia cultivar (F. magellanica 'Variegata'), which has gray foliage tinged with maroon.

When choosing a color scheme for your garden, it is important to consider contrasts and harmonies. These are best understood by visualizing an artist's color wheel. First, arrange the three primary colors—red, blue, and yellow—in a circle. Then blend each primary color with its neighbor to create the secondary colors—purple, green, and orange. From these six colors, hundreds of other colors can be created.

In the shade garden you have a tremendous palette with which to work. All of the primary and secondary colors can be represented by at least one flower. Foliage also comes in many colors.

Colors that are close to one another on the color wheel, such as pinks and purples, are called harmonious colors. Colors opposite each other, such as blues and oranges, are known as contrasting colors.

Beyond the pure colors, there are many tints and shades created by the addition of white or black. Pure white has a handsome brilliancy on its own, but it softens any hue to which it is added, creating a pastel color. Pastels are especially prevalent among flowers that bloom in the shade.

Before you consider color schemes for the garden and decide whether you want to feature harmonious or contrasting hues, study the garden site. Is it dark and gloomy or bright and airy? Dark colors will be lost in a fully shaded woodland but will add contrast in a bright clearing with dappled sun. Gleaming whites and other light colors do well in both situations. Pastels may shine softly in the dark but look washed out in a brighter location.

Another option is to create a monochromatic garden with all the flowers in shades of a single color. Monochromatic schemes are particularly effective in

Colored plant foliage is a wonderful component in a shade garden setting. Here, the lime-green and white leaves of spotted dead nettle (Lamium maculatum 'Aurea') add a band of brilliant color to a setting without any blossoms.

Hosta foliage comes in so many different colors and forms that shade gardeners can create elegant compositions with just this single plant genus.

Testing Colors
If you're unsure whether a color is right for your garden, first plant annual flowers in the hue of your choice. If the color works, the next year you can plant more permanent shrubs, bulbs, or perennials.

If you like variety, plan on including some annuals in the garden every year, and change their colors each season. Choose perennials and shrubs with white blossoms, which will go with whatever annuals you wish to grow.

shade because there is such a wide range of foliage shapes and textures with which to work. Some foliage combinations are so beautiful—such as the dusky blue of the vase-shaped *Hosta* 'Krossa Regal' paired with the feathery gray- and maroon-tinged fronds of the Japanese painted fern *(Athyrium goeringianum* 'Pictum')—that you may well want to eliminate any further color intrusions.

A garden of white flowers, complemented by blue, warm green, or even red-tinged foliage, is very effective in a shady setting, whether the shade is heavy or bright. This kind of garden can have flowers from spring through fall. It could begin, for example, with the gleaming white petals of bloodroot *(Sanguinaria canadensis)*, which open in early spring, when the ground is still covered with last year's dead leaves. Follow the bloodroot with white crested iris *(I. cristata* 'Alba'), a lovely woodland native. Both these plants have good-looking, contrasting foliage. The bloodroot has large, lobed leaves, while the iris has short, swordlike leaves. For summer, plant clumps of variegated hosta *(H. undulata)*, which has large, smooth, green-and-white leaves, near groups of Deutschland astilbe *(A. × arendsii* 'Deutschland'), with its dark green, fernlike foliage and plumes of bright white flowers. Place bright white impatiens wherever there is room. And for a grand finale, tuck in several white-flowered hardy begonias *(Begonia grandis* 'Alba'). These plants have large leaves tinged with red on the underside and bear lovely drooping white flowers from spring to fall.

If you like bolder statements, you might choose red impatiens and astilbes instead of white, and plant bright yellow celandine poppies *(Stylophorum diphyllum)* and yellow corydalis *(C. lutea)* in place of the bloodroot and crested iris described above. Instead of the hardy begonias, scatter pots of orange and red tuberous begonias around the garden.

If you like gently harmonious colors, use the soft blues of the wild sweet William *(Phlox divaricata)*, the lovely pinks of bleeding-hearts *(Dicentra eximia* and *D. formosa)*, and the pale yellow of the Pagoda fawn lily *(Erythronium* 'Pagoda') in spring. Follow with the summer-long pale pink flowers of the Lancaster geranium *(G. sanguineum* var. *striatum)*, the large but soft pink leaves of various caladiums, and the blue spikes of monkshood *(Aconitum* spp.). Conclude the garden year with the chalice-shaped, soft pink flowers of *Colchicum* cultivars such as C. 'Waterlily'.

Shapes and Textures

Dwarf Evergreens

Small evergreen shrubs provide structure and interest in the shade garden throughout the year. The yellow-flowered shrubby St.-John's-wort (Hypericum prolificum)*, the dark-pink-blossomed mountain laurel* (Kalmia latifolia *'Elf'*), *and dwarf Japanese hollies* (Ilex crenata *'Helleri' and 'Tiny Tim'*) *are particularly choice examples of plants that require minimal maintenance.*

*U*nusual shapes make wonderful accents in a garden. Some plants assume such shapes naturally. The glossy chartreuse-to-gold leaves of *Hosta* 'Sum and Substance', for example, form a smooth, rounded clump 5 feet wide and just over 2 feet tall. Other plants take readily to clipping. Hollies, especially Meserve holly *(Ilex × meserveae)* and American holly *(I. opaca)*, are often trimmed into topiaries.

When overused, however, unusual shapes can overpower a garden design. Employ them sparingly, primarily as accents in a selected area.

Combining textures, on the other hand, is essential to successful shade garden design. Think of texture in terms of a plant's overall appearance and the form of its foliage. To assess texture, step back to see if the plant is bold or delicate. Bear's-breech *(Acanthus mollis)*, for example, is a stately plant with such large

leaves that it almost resembles a shrub. If you tucked one delicate maidenhair fern *(Adiantum pedatum)* next to a bear's-breech, the fern would be lost. But a large grouping of maidenhair ferns would complement one bear's-breech.

Plant leaves can be bold or delicate and dull or shiny. These contrasts can be lovely in a border. For instance, you might surround the large, rough leaves of Siberian bugloss *(Brunnera macrophylla)* with the lustrous, glossy leaves of European wild ginger *(Asarum europaeum)*.

Texture contrasts are particularly useful in small borders. Coarse textures appear to come forward, while fine textures recede. Thus, a small, narrow shade garden looks much deeper if you put large-leaved plants, such as bergenias, in front and taller plants with smaller leaves, such as astilbes, in back.

Hay-scented ferns (Dennstaedtia punctilobula) *are not only easy to grow but also offer a bonus of brilliant color in the fall shade garden.*

The Japanese painted fern (Athyrium goeringianum *'Pictum'*) *contributes cool, elegant beauty to shade gardens with its ghostly silver fronds and purple-tinged ribs.*

The bold shape of hosta foliage adds a sculptural ingredient to a garden. As an extra bonus, these versatile shade plants bear white or lavender flowers, which contrast nicely with the foliage.

Though most shade gardeners admire bloodroots (Sanguinaria canadensis) *for their brilliant white spring flowers, some like the bold, lobed, and notched green leaves even better. You might try using the strong foliage of this plant to complement the light, lustrous leaves of astilbes.*

Pachysandra has whorled leaves with irregular edges that are emphasized by a creamy outline in the variegated form. The light edging gives the plant more visual weight in a dimly lit setting.

Shaded City Garden

A formal or semiformal design sometimes works best for a shaded city garden. The curved lines of the beds and the graceful use of a garden ornament, the pedestal planter, give this small space form and beauty in all seasons.

If you have a fence or wall surrounding your property, plant vines to add a vertical dimension to the greenery. The shrubs in this urban oasis are graceful fetterbush, at the right rear, and beautiful mountain laurel on the front left. Hostas provide large, leafy accents throughout the growing season.

Plant List

1 Daffodil
(Narcissus pseudonarcissus)
2 Mountain laurel
(Kalmia latifolia)
3 Carpet bugleweed
(Ajuga reptans)
4 Hosta
(Hosta sieboldiana)
5 Fetterbush
(Leucothoe fontanesiana)
6 Japanese painted fern
(Athyrium goeringianum 'Pictum'*)*
7 Wax begonia
(Begonia × semperflorens-cultorum)
8 English ivy
(Hedera helix)

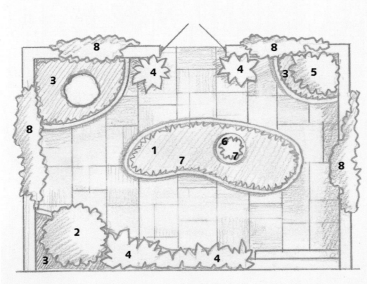

Bugleweed is an easy-care ground cover that grows well, even in problem areas, such as under trees and shrubs in this garden. Trying to grow grass in these areas would be a big mistake!

Highlighting this serene, shady courtyard is an island bed that features golden daffodils in spring. When the daffodils fade they can be planted over with colorful begonias. Or you can over-plant the daffodils with annuals that will hide the dying daffodil foliage and will provide summer color to the island bed. Begonias can also be planted in the pedestal planter with ferns when the weather becomes warm enough.

Cool Passage

The large, striking ostrich fern fronds can grow up to 5 feet tall. They grow best in moist areas with soil rich in organic matter. Under ideal conditions, ostrich ferns will spread by underground runners, but the plants can easily be weeded back to maintain their position in this garden.

*T*his arbor shelters a path leading into a hot, sunny garden. Underneath the shade of the arbor is an abundance of cool greenery, with graceful ferns and dramatic big-leaved elephant's-ear plants as well as white-leaved fancy caladiums. Pink begonias add a touch of warm color to the foliage of the plants.

On many sweltering days, this cool passage with its marble bench is more appealing than the sunny garden beyond. The lattice panels admit breezes and enough light for the plants to flourish. Astilbes and big blue lilyturfs guard the entrance to this shaded retreat, and ivy grows up the trellis to provide even more protection from the hot sun.

Plant List

1 Astilbe
(Astilbe × arendsii)
2 Big blue lilyturf
(Liriope muscari)
3 Wax begonia
(Begonia × semperflorens-cultorum)
4 Brake fern
(Pteris cretica)
5 Fancy-leaved caladium
(Caladium × hortulanum)
6 Elephant's-ear plant
(Alocasia indica)
7 Ostrich fern
(Matteuccia struthiopteris)
8 English ivy
(Hedera helix)

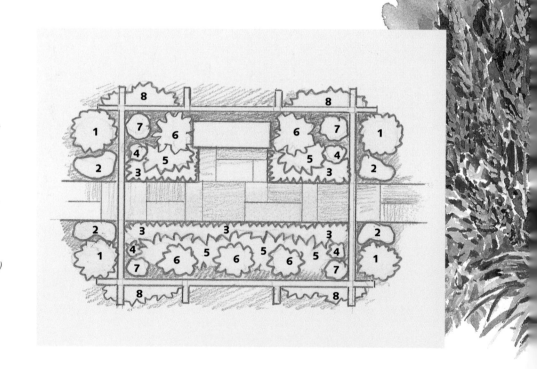

Enchanted Forest

*T*his garden takes advantage of a wonderful combination: an existing wood with a brook running through it. A path wanders into the woods on one side of the garden. Stepping stones lead across the creek, and a pine-needle trail circles around—through plantings of hepatica, phlox, and creeping Jennie—to a lovely arching bridge surrounded by ferns.

Primulas and Virginia bluebells bloom along the path, providing a colorful contrast to the fallen pine needles. Tread softly as you meander through this lovely setting to avoid disturbing the wildlife that is sure to be attracted to this garden.

Even if you don't have a brook or such an elaborate bridge on your property, you can create the feeling of this garden in any wooded area. Design a meandering path from your backyard through a shaded area and back again, trying to make use of any existing trails to avoid disturbing the natural habitat as much as possible. Then use similar plants to those in this garden. Your forest will be just as enchanting as the one shown here.

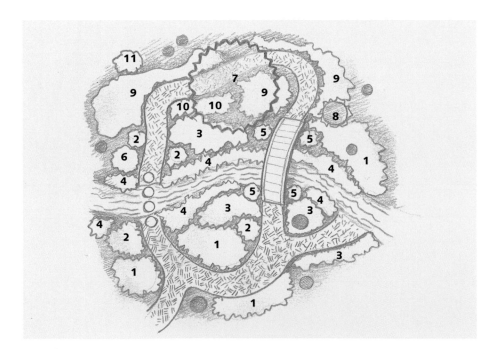

Plant List
1 Virginia bluebells
(*Mertensia virginica*)
2 Sharp-lobed hepatica
(*Hepatica acutiloba*)
3 Cowslip
(*Primula veris*)
4 Creeping Jennie
(*Lysimachia nummularia*)
5 Hay-scented fern
(*Dennstaedtia punctilobula*)
6 Christmas fern
(*Polystichum acrostichoides*)
7 Flowering dogwood
(*Cornus × rutgersensis*)
8 Paperbark maple
(*Acer griseum*)
9 Blue phlox
(*Phlox divaricata*)
10 Wild bleeding-heart
(*Dicentra eximia*)
11 Cinnamon fern
(*Osmunda cinnamomea*)

Bird Sanctuary

*I*f you have a beautiful shade tree with nothing growing under it, here is a garden that will transform it into a fragrant, colorful thicket with plenty of hiding places for birds and other wildlife.

The look of this wildlife haven is soft and lacy, inviting you to settle nearby with bird books, notebooks, and binoculars. You'll enjoy the blooms in this garden from late spring through early summer or midsummer.

Plant List

1 Green-and-gold
(Chrysogonum virginianum)
2 Forget-me-not
(Myosotis scorpioides)
3 Exbury hybrid azalea
(Rhododendron hybrid*)*
4 Sweet pepperbush
(Clethra alnifolia 'Pink
Spires'*)*
5 Monkshood
(Aconitum carmichaelii)
6 Virginia sweetspire
(Itea virginica)
7 Korean spice viburnum
(Viburnum carlesii)
8 Carolina silverbell
(Halesia carolina)
9 Existing large shade tree

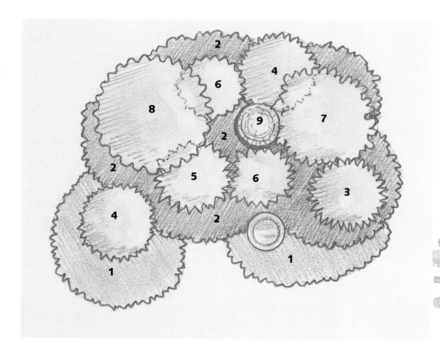

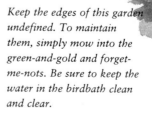

Keep the edges of this garden undefined. To maintain them, simply mow into the green-and-gold and forget-me-nots. Be sure to keep the water in the birdbath clean and clear.

The Korean spice viburnum bears large, fragrant flowers in spring. The flowers are followed in summer by blue blackberries, which birds love to eat.

CHAPTER 2

Managing a Shaded Environment

Shade is not an immutable phenomenon. You can create it, lessen it, or eliminate it altogether. Even without your active intervention, the amount of light in any garden area changes over time. Trees get taller, fences fall down, and new buildings are constructed. • All of this activity can affect your shade-loving plants. This chapter reviews step-by-step how you can work with a shaded environment to create a lovely garden full of healthy plants. We'll show you how to select plants for your shaded landscape, how to modify your property to change the light conditions, and how to grow lovely shade plants despite difficult growing situations. • You'll also learn how to modify your soil to create the ideal growing medium for your shade-tolerant plants.

Choosing Shade-Tolerant Plants

One of the biggest gardening myths is that it's hard to create a colorful shade garden. The encyclopedia beginning on page 96 of this book certainly refutes such thinking by describing more than 150 colorful plants that need some shade in order to look their best. These plants bear beautiful flowers in hues ranging from orange or bright yellow to lavender, and some have magnificent foliage streaked with pink, purple, silver, or gold. Truly, the shade garden palette is a rich one.

Start your selection of plants by examining shrubs that do well in shade. The flowers of azaleas, rhododendrons, and mountain laurels are popular spring decorations. Hydrangeas and sweet pepperbush *(Clethra alnifolia)* bloom during the summer. *Clethra* is a particular favorite because it is sweetly fragrant and perfumes many a late-summer afternoon or evening with its beguiling scent. For ongoing foliage interest, choose shrubs such as gold-dust plant *(Aucuba japonica* 'Gold-Dust') and a variegated Japanese lily-of-the-valley bush *(Pieris japonica* 'Variegata').

Consider perennials next. Perennials die back to the ground in winter but reappear in your garden year after year without replanting. Three shade garden staples—ferns, hostas, and astilbes—are perennials. These popular shade plants provide colorful flowers, attractive foliage, and textural contrasts in the garden. Hundreds of other perennials also stand out in shaded settings. When choosing perennials, consider the season of bloom and try to incorporate plants that flower in summer and fall, as well as spring.

Many perennials do not emerge from their winter dormancy until mid- to late spring. Similarly, several

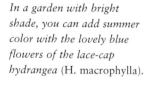

In a garden with bright shade, you can add summer color with the lovely blue flowers of the lace-cap hydrangea (H. macrophylla).

The dainty white flowers of lily-of-the-valley (Convallaria majalis) *offer springtime fragrance. A vigorous ground cover, lily-of-the-valley spreads rapidly in good soil.*

Tender Bulbs

The following bulbs, all grown as annuals in most parts of the United States and in Canada, are perfect for containers placed in dark, shady spots. The tuberous begonia (B. Tuberhybrida hybrids) bears large, lustrous flowers in soft pastels as well as bright oranges and vibrant reds. Caladium (C. × hortulanum) foliage is spectacular, splashed with various shades of white, pink, and red. Lily-of-the-Nile (Agapanthus orientalis), a plant which is especially suited to urban environments, bears lovely trumpet-shaped flowers in blue or white.

deciduous shrubs are late to leaf out. To fill in the bare spots that will eventually be covered by foliage later in spring, consider small early-blooming bulbs. Many, such as snowdrops *(Galanthus nivalis)* and winter aconites *(Eranthis hyemalis),* need bare ground basking in winter sun and then the protective, cool covering of foliage in summer.

Other bulbs, particularly lilies, add drama and elegance to a summer border. Two outstanding charmers, meadow lily *(Lilium canadense)* and Turk's-cap lily *(L. superbum),* are natives that grow in shady places throughout the eastern United States.

Some bulbs are truly movable feasts. They grow beautifully in containers, which can be moved during the garden year. Display the plants when they bloom, then put them out of sight when they finish. The blue

or white flowers and handsome, straplike green foliage of African lily *(Agapanthus africanus)* thrive in large pots in city gardens or on north-facing patios or decks in the suburbs.

Caladiums are wonderful bulbs for shade gardens. They can be planted directly in the soil or in containers. Their large, colorful leaves will brighten the garden all summer.

If you still have bare spots in your garden once you have placed your shrubs, perennials, and bulbs, fill the gaps with colorful annuals such as impatiens and begonias. These shallow-rooted, long-blooming fillers are particularly good for covering spots where spring bulbs and perennials once bloomed but have become dormant by summer.

Modifying Shade

*I*f you have deep shade, such as the kind existing in the heart of a thick woodland or in a city courtyard surrounded by tall buildings, the selection of plants you can grow is quite limited. To broaden your possibilities, you must change the light conditions. Depending on the situation, this can be done by increasing reflectors or eliminating blockages.

Given the opportunity, light will bounce around. Bright objects, such as white walls or fences, pathways of light-colored pebbles, or even strategically placed mirrors or reflecting balls, will capture any available light and shoot it off in different directions. Many plants, including epimediums, hardy begonias, and primulas, will grow splendidly in reflected light even if they receive no direct sun at all.

To alter the light in your garden, incorporate one or more of the reflectors mentioned above. Where possible, add two, such as a white fence and light stones. Using reflectors greatly increases your plant choices, while still allowing you the luxury of gardening in the cool shade.

Obviously, if you are a city person, you can't just tear down the buildings that are blocking your light. You have to add reflectors to your garden or search for plants that grow in deep shade. But if the shade in your garden is created by trees, you can brighten your garden and expand your plant choices by having a professional selectively remove or trim your trees.

Check the evergreens first. Do they add interest to the garden, or are they simply large, dark structures? Evergreens that are not particularly attractive and create hostile root environments for other plants, such as eastern white pine *(Pinus strobus),* are prime candidates for removal. Other evergreens, such as Douglas

1 *To add light to a setting shaded by trees, trim the lower branches with a long-handled pruner. You will also improve the look of the trees.*

firs *(Pseudotsuga menziesii),* can be trimmed—limbed" is the word arborists use—to remove lower branches (as high as 40 feet) and let in light and air.

Deciduous trees can also have their lower branches trimmed. Fortunately, many of these trees are naturally airy and let light ripple through their canopies. If the shade canopy from your trees is quite dense, however, you can always hire a professional to thin the higher branches for you.

1 Painting a dark gray fence white is an attractive way to brighten up a shade border. Protect the plants underneath with a cover while you are painting.

2 Another easy solution to lightening up a shady area is to add a mulch of white stones. The white color reflects light onto the surrounding plants.

A dark spot is lightened by a pale wall, allowing plants that enjoy a little sun, such as tuberous begonias, firethorn (Pyracantha), and lilyturf (Ophiopogon planis-capus 'Nigrescens'), to become lush and healthy even in the shade.

The Environment Underground

*T*hough shade flowers evolved in woodland settings, not all forests contain such plants. Pine forests, for example, often feature floors that are barren except for fallen needles. The highly acidic needles create a hostile environment for plants that otherwise would do well in shade.

In addition, trees with shallow, invasive roots may discourage flowering plants. European beeches *(Fagus sylvatica)* and black locusts *(Robinia pseudoacacia)* are particularly notorious in this regard. Their roots scurry along right under the topmost layer of soil, gobbling up nutrients and available water.

To alleviate poor growing conditions in the underground environment of your garden, try one or more of the following ideas:

▼ Build a raised bed. Using railroad ties or stones, create a planting area that is at least 6 inches high.

Fill this with a mix of humus, sand, and loam, then incorporate your plants.

▼ Try container gardening. Spread porous sand over the roots in the area you wish to garden. Smooth it out so that the ground is level and the roots are hidden by the sand. (If you use a light-colored sand, you can increase reflection in the garden.) Next, place containers on the level growing area. Fill them with a good all-purpose potting mix, then plant.

▼ Create a patio. If the tree roots take too much time and effort to combat, simply pave over the area to create a cool summer retreat. You can make this spot especially colorful by filling it with flowering plants in containers.

1 *When the underground environment is extremely hostile or space is limited, container plants provide an easy, attractive solution.*

2 *If shallow roots make it impossible to plant a tree, create a ring garden with potted plants. Vary the containers and the plants for a striking setting.*

1 A raised bed filled with ferns is structurally and horticulturally interesting as well as low in maintenance. First choose a height for the shade-tolerant bed.

2 Once you have constructed the edge for your border, clear away all weeds and then fill in the area with loamy soil. Try to include leaf mold in the soil mix.

3 After the soil has been leveled and allowed to settle a day or two, position the potted ferns. Experiment with different arrangements and compositions to see what you like.

4 Once you are satisfied with your design, remove the ferns from their pots and place them in the prepared bed. Make sure the planting holes are large enough.

5 After each fern has been planted, gently firm the soil in place. This step requires some care, as fern fronds are fragile and can break easily. Don't worry if a few break; new ones grow quickly.

6 Carefully water each fern after it has been planted. To discourage spores from germinating, add a thick, attractive mulch. Do not mulch if you want the ferns to spread.

Creating Shade

Shade Trees

The following trees combine large canopies with deep taproots, creating ideal conditions for growing understory plants in shade: bitternut hickory (Carya cordiformis), *common hackberry* (Celtis occidentalis 'Prairie Prince'), *white oak* (Quercus alba), *American linden* (Tilia americana), *and Japanese zelkova* (Z. serrata 'Village Green').

Not all gardeners are fortunate enough to have some shady areas in which to grow plants. Southern gardeners in particular have to cope with this acute lack because plants that are sun lovers in other parts of the country must have at least some cooling shade in the South to protect them from the intense sun and unremitting heat.

There are several ways to create shade if you need to. One way is to plant trees. However, large trees are expensive to purchase and install. Unless you have a lot of money, you will have to wait for the trees to grow to obtain adequate shade. Choose trees that grow fast and have a light canopy and deep roots, such as the Shademaster thornless honey locust *(Gleditsia triacanthos* var. *inermis* 'Shademaster').

If your property is not large enough to plant several trees, consider growing smaller trees in containers.

With some effort, using a dolly or other assistance, you can move these to accommodate changing light conditions and create "portable" shade. Good container candidates include Amur maple *(Acer ginnala)*, Russian olive *(Elaeagnus angustifolia)*, and box elder *(Acer negundo)*. Tree-of-heaven *(Ailanthus altissima)* is considered a weed in many urban areas but provides good shade when restrained in a container.

Another way to create shade is to build fences. While zoning laws often restrict its height, a fence can at least create shade for a narrow border on its north side. Fences are a handsome architectural feature in a garden, and you can construct them from many different kinds of materials (including plants).

Another architectural way to create shade is to build or buy an arbor, pergola, or lath house. These are often simple and beautiful structures.

Trumpet vine (Campsis radicans) *will quickly cover an arbor and provide both brilliant orange-red flowers and cool shade through the hot summer months. Make sure this and other fast-growing perennial vines are contained at their roots, as they can be invasive.*

1 A leaf tunnel is a living architectural pathway in a woodland garden. To start one, first prune low limbs on trees to allow dappled light to filter through the branches.

2 Next, clear the walking area for the tunnel. Remove small weeds by hand or with a trowel. Be sure to clear all roots completely so that they will not resprout.

3 Once the smaller weeds are removed, it is time to attack any light underbrush. You'll need a weed trimmer to accomplish this task. Bag and remove all debris.

4 Use a grubbing tool to remove any plant materials not cleared by the weed trimmer. Remove all underbrush roots.

5 To facilitate removal of trees from the area, carefully chop small trees with an ax, as shown here, and dig out the roots.

6 Once the leaf tunnel has been created, clear the ground underneath with a rake. If necessary, add soil or compost prior to planting.

Getting Plants Out of the Shade

Vines

Climbing clematis vines are excellent plants for areas with shade at ground level and sun higher up. Three outstanding vines to choose are Jackman clematis (C. × jackmanii), which has purplish violet flowers from summer through frost; sweet autumn clematis (C. maximowicziana), which has profuse white flowers in late summer; and Betty Corning clematis (C. viticella 'Betty Corning'), which has bicolored silver-and-blue flowers that appear in spring and then often rebloom in fall.

Sometimes it's possible to "cheat" when you have a shade garden. There are various ways to sneak plants from dark places out into sunshine.

Clematis vines provide a good example. Clematis likes to have its roots and stem bases moist and cooled by shade. On the other hand, its flowers generally like full sun. The perfect spot for clematis is under a shrub or at the foot of a trellis, where the roots are in shade while the top growth climbs toward the sunlight.

Most early-blooming bulbs like to be out of the shade when they flower, which you can accomplish by planting them under deciduous trees. Daffodils *(Narcissus* spp.*)* and Spanish bluebells *(Endymion hispanicus)* will create a colorful spring carpet of white, yellow, pink, and blue on sunny woodland floors that are cloaked in shade by the time summer arrives.

Several perennials also thrive in such situations. The glistening white flowers of bloodroot *(Sanguinaria canadensis)*, for example, do fine in full sun in early spring but must have shade throughout the remainder of the garden year.

In shady conditions, container gardening can also produce both flower cuttings and vegetable harvests. Plants such as lettuce, radishes, spinach, and onions can all be grown in containers and moved about as the sunlight pattern in the area changes. Since these vegetables can tolerate some shade—particularly bright shade—for a while, you should not need to move them too frequently.

Many vines, such as the hybrid honeysuckle (Lonicera × tellmanniana) *pictured here, can be planted at the shady base of an arbor to keep their roots cool while the foliage clambers up toward the sun.*

Soil

*T*hroughout the world, thousands of plants thrive in the shade of trees. The natural habitat of these plants is one with soil rich in the organic matter created by fallen leaves and rotted trunks. To grow such plants, you need to duplicate the fertile, light, humusy, and slightly acidic soil of a woodland site in your garden.

If your property is wooded, such soil may already exist. If that woodland is filled with shallow-rooted trees, however, remedial action is generally recommended. First, make a soil mixture of two parts humus (compost, leaf mold, or peat moss) to one part builder's sand and one part clay soil. The humus makes the soil light and porous while increasing water retention, the sand ensures good drainage, and the clay provides nutrients.

If you wish to plant directly in the ground, spread a 6-inch-deep layer of the soil mixture from the trunk of the tree to about 5 feet beyond the drip line. Then, using a sharp spade, thoroughly work the mixture into the existing soil. As you dig, chop off the tree roots with the edge of your spade and remove them. By adding soil and clearing roots, you will give the flowers you plant a chance to establish themselves.

If this seems like too much work, you can construct a raised bed for your plants. Make the raised beds at least 6 inches deep, and fill them with the soil mix.

Some shade gardens may be located on the north side of a house or condominium building in newly developed areas that have been stripped of their topsoil. In the Southwest the available soil may be dry and very alkaline. In either case, spread a 6-inch layer of soil mixture and work it in thoroughly. In alkaline soil you may have to add sulfur to lower the pH to a more acceptable range for plants.

Azaleas, hostas, and mayapples thrive in woodlands, where falling leaves decay and provide the loamy, acidic, and well-drained soil they need.

Soil CONTINUED

1 *Leaf mold is an excellent—and inexpensive— additive to soil. First, rake leaves into a pile. Use a tarp, as shown here, to haul the leaves to the composting site.*

2 *After the leaves have been collected, use a mulching mower or shredder to grind them. Ground-up leaves decompose faster and will be ready to use by spring.*

3 *Use chicken wire or other material to make a holding bin for the leaves. The openness of the wire allows air to circulate and hastens decomposition of the leaves.*

4 *After the leaves have been shredded, dump them into the bin. Lightly spraying each layer with water will speed decomposition, but this procedure is not necessary.*

5 *By the following spring, you should have beautiful, rich brown leaf mold to spread about your garden beds. It will continue to decompose and will enrich your soil.*

Other Factors

A Japanese maple, pachysandras, and ferns thrive in the shade of a cool-climate garden. Such a lovely scene would not be possible in the hot, dry conditions of the Southwest.

*I*n managing your shade garden environment, also consider moisture, temperature, and plant spacing.

Shade plants like moisture in the air but do not need to be watered as frequently as plants in sunny gardens. This seeming contradiction arises because moisture evaporates more quickly in an open, sunny location than in a cool, shady spot.

When watering is required, do it early in the day to allow the maximum amount of time for moisture to evaporate from plant foliage before evening. Water droplets remaining on leaves after dark are often an invitation to fungal and viral diseases.

Temperature affects the growth of shade lovers. These shade plants like cool growing conditions—that's why they're shade plants! Remember that morning sun is cool, appearing after night has ban-

ished much of the previous day's heat. Afternoon sun, however, shines when heat has been building up. Thus, many shade plants do fine with a half-day of morning sun but cannot survive a half-day of afternoon sun. If your plants receive morning shade and afternoon sun, mulch well and provide plenty of water to help offset the heat.

Finally, be sensitive to the space needs of shade plants. Plants tend to spread out more in shade to capture the maximum amount of light, so leave enough space between them. If crowded, shade plants tend to become weak and spindly. If you are in doubt over proper spacing, opt for a wider-than-usual distance between perennials, and fill in any bare spots later with annuals.

CHAPTER 3

Planting and Propagating

*O*nce you've created a plan for your garden and chosen plants that will not only implement your design but also thrive in your garden's environment, it is time to transform your dreams and planning into reality. This chapter is filled with step-by-step instructions on the proper way to install different kinds of shade plants. • The chapter concludes with information on the many different ways to propagate your plants. • By following this advice, you may soon find yourself with abundant plants for your own garden and many more to give to friends and family.

Sowing Seeds

Growing plants from seeds is the cheapest and, in many cases, the easiest way to obtain lovely flowers and foliage plants for the shady garden. In many gardens a number of plants, such as perennial Jacob's-ladder *(Polemonium* spp.*)*, celandine poppies *(Stylophorum diphyllum)*, annual impatiens, wax begonias, biennial foxgloves *(Digitalis* spp.*)*, and forget-me-nots *(Myosotis scorpioides)*, will reseed on their own. Gardening really can't get easier than that!

The self-sowing habits of these flowers illustrate how you should seed most shade plants. In general, seeds of spring-blooming perennial flowers germinate by midsummer. By fall, seedlings are scattered about the garden and can easily be transplanted to places where you want them. This pattern is extremely helpful to busy gardeners, who like to put off sowing seeds until late June or July, when other planting activities in the garden are relatively quiet.

Seeds from summer- and fall-blooming perennials, however, usually do not germinate until the following spring. For these flowers, April or May is the time of year to plant seeds outdoors in most parts of the United States. Gardeners in warm climates can plant a bit earlier. Transplant the seedlings to their desired locations in the fall, or if that is too busy a time of year for you, wait until the following spring.

Some hardy annuals will self-sow if they are not deadheaded; others can be sown in fall. But annual seeds that overwinter outdoors often do not germinate until late spring, especially in the North. By the time the plants start to bloom, the growing season may be almost over. Generally it's best for gardeners north of zone 6 to start annual seeds indoors in the late-winter months. With the weather usually so dreary outside, it's fun to be growing plants indoors.

Sowing seeds indoors is a great way to forget about the bleakness of winter outdoors. It is also the least costly way to obtain plants for your shade garden.

1 *Money plant (Lunaria annua) is a low-care shade biennial that is easy to grow from seed. Simply clear the planting area, making sure weeds are removed.*

2 *Money plant is a self-seeder, so follow its example when introducing it into your garden. Simply sprinkle seeds about on bare soil, just as the plant would naturally.*

3 *To make sure the seeds are not blown or washed away, press them firmly into the soil. You can use a rake, as shown here, or simply walk firmly over the planting area.*

4 *Gently water the seedbed, taking care that the seeds do not wash together. In this way, you won't waste time thinning out sprouted clumps later.*

Sowing Seeds CONTINUED

It is important to time indoor plantings correctly so that your annual flowers do not outgrow their indoor homes before it is time to plant them out in the garden. Seedlings kept indoors too long will be weak; they will grow slowly and bloom poorly. Be sure to check the instructions on the seed packet before sowing seeds indoors. These directions will tell you when to start the seeds indoors and when to plant the seedlings outdoors. Wishbone flower *(Torenia fournieri)*, for example, should be started indoors 10 to 12 weeks before your last frost date. Seeds for polka-dot plant *(Hypoestes phyllostachya)*, on the other hand, are sown just six weeks before the last frost date.

Biennials, as the name implies, need two seasons in order to bloom in the shade garden. Many biennials self-sow after blooming in their second season if you do not deadhead them. The self-sown seeds germinate by the end of the growing season. Since the new seedlings are young and do not have extended root systems, they can easily be transplanted to where you would like them to grow in the garden. The seedlings then need to overwinter before they will produce flowers in their second growing season. As with spring-blooming perennials, you can sow seeds of biennials as late as midsummer.

Because seeds have different light requirements and different germination times, it is important to read the instructions on the seed packet, particularly when you are starting plants indoors. Make sure you separate the containers according to the plants' light requirements and germination times, keeping pots of plants with similar needs together.

TROUBLESHOOTING TIP

Handling the seeds of some shade plants can be difficult (a million begonia seeds weigh just an ounce!). One way to ease planting is to mix these seeds with white table sugar or fine sand and then stir to distribute the seeds evenly. Use a spoon to spread the mixture over the planting medium. The sugar or sand will not harm the seeds and will dissolve in the soil when watered.

1 *When impatiens self-seed, they do not flower until late summer. To give this annual an early start indoors, sprinkle seeds on top of a moistened soil mix.*

5 *Cover the prepared seed tray with a plastic container. This will prevent water evaporation, thus keeping the soil constantly moist, and at the same time allow light through.*

2 With your fingertips, gently press the seeds into place in the soil. Make sure the planting mixture is level. Next, barely cover the seeds with dry soil mix.

3 When planting more than one variety, clearly label each seed tray. Use white plastic markers and pens with indelible ink, available at garden centers and hardware stores.

4 Plants grown indoors are often troubled by a fungal disease known as damping-off. To guard against this problem, spray the seed tray with a fungicide.

6 Once the seeds have germinated and true leaves (the second set) appear, transfer the seedlings to their own pots. Separate the seedlings carefully so as not to harm the roots.

7 Harden off the seedlings in a cold frame. There, protected from winds and insects, they become acclimated to temperature and light fluctuations outdoors.

8 Your homegrown seedlings should be compact and stocky, as shown on the right; they should not look like the lanky plant held on the left.

Planting Annuals and Perennials

*A*nnual and perennial transplants come in all sizes and shapes—from a 1-inch impatiens seedling in a plastic cell pack to a 3-foot-tall summer phlox in a 2-gallon container. The technique used for transplanting is determined by the size of the plant and how it is contained.

No matter what size plant you are working with, take time to prepare a proper planting hole for each new addition to the garden. Make the hole slightly larger than the space occupied by the roots of the plant you are putting in. Unless you are planting bog plants, make sure that there is good drainage in your planting area. (To check drainage, dig a planting hole and pour in a bucket of water; if the water drains off within 15 minutes, drainage is good.) In addition, be prepared to water liberally right after transplanting and for several days or weeks afterward. Keep the soil

evenly moist (but not soggy) while the plants become established in the garden and begin to grow new roots. Keep the planting area free of weeds.

We have already discussed how to transplant self-sown seedlings (see pages 52–55), and transplanting bulbs and perennials that have been divided is explained on pages 75–80. Below are some guidelines on installing plants you have purchased through the mail or at a local garden center or nursery.

▼ Bare-Root Plants

Due to interstate shipping restrictions, many plants sent through the mail are not allowed to be packed in soil of any kind. Other plants are so large that the addition of soil in the packaging would make shipping costs too expensive. For these reasons, when you buy plants through the mail, you may find yourself

Colorful biennial forget-me-nots (Myosotis sylvatica) *are prolific producers of seed. If there is open ground nearby for the seed to fall upon, you will have self-sown spring bouquets of these plants every year.*

1 *It's a delight to discover that some beautiful plants readily seed themselves in the garden. Here are some self-sown Lenten rose (*Helleborus orientalis*) seedlings.*

2 *Because these seedlings are so crammed together, they are already stressed. Dig them out very gently with a trowel. Be careful not to damage the small, delicate roots.*

3 *Replant the seedlings immediately. To provide the best growing conditions, add generous amounts of leaf mold to the soil. Gently firm the soil around each plant, then water.*

confronted with a plant that looks almost dead, wrapped in some kind of damp organic material. Do not despair. Many plants are shipped while they are dormant, with the bare roots enclosed in a lightweight packing material.

As soon as you receive a shipment from a mailorder nursery, carefully unwrap the material around the roots and, if possible, soak the roots in water for an hour or two. While the roots are getting a drink, prepare the planting holes. Make each hole a bit deeper than the height of the plant roots (look for a soil line on the stem, or look for the crown, the point at which the roots meet the main stem). Make a mound of loose soil in the middle of the hole. Next, set the plant on the mound and carefully spread the roots over the mound. Check the depth—the crown should be right at the soil level when the hole is filled

so that the plant sits at the same depth at which it was planted in the nursery field. Fill the hole with soil, working it around the roots with your fingers. Water to settle the soil, then add more soil to fill any holes that remain. You will probably see green shoots emerging from the crown within a week or so.

▼ Plastic Cell Packs

Cell packs, or "six-packs," are popular plant containers at both local and mail-order nurseries. When shopping for plants at local garden centers, look for cell packs that have plants still in bud rather than in bloom—they will adapt more quickly after transplanting. Also, check to make sure that the plants appear sturdy and stocky and that the foliage is healthy, with good color.

Planting Annuals and Perennials CONTINUED

Planting is very easy. Simply cut or rip open one of the cells, or press on the bottom to loosen the plant. Gently slide out the plant, soil mix and all. Check to see if the roots are tangled or densely packed. If they are, loosen them or cut into the bottom of the root ball to split it. You won't hurt the plant; this kind of treatment will encourage the plant to send new roots out into the soil. Set the plant into the prepared planting hole. Firmly press the soil into place around it. The plant should sit at the same depth at which it was growing in the cell pack. Because they hold lots of seedlings, undivided flats or packs containing many plants are enticing at the garden center. But this kind of crowding is often detrimental to a plant's health. In addition, it leads to tangled roots, which must be separated before individual plants can be put into the ground. Generally, there is less potting soil available for each individual seedling, and you must be very careful that you do not damage any of the roots.

If the seedling roots are all grown together, a few days before planting cut the soil into blocks with a sharp knife so that each seedling sits in its own block of soil. If seedlings are not so tightly packed, you can remove one or more at a time and gently disentangle the roots. When you have separated a plant from the group in the container, hold it above the plant hole and slowly lower it so that the top of the root mass is just below soil level. Then, while still holding the plant, gently sprinkle in soil until the plant is firmly in place. Planting depth is especially critical for plants that grow from a single point (and form a rosette of leaves that sits on top of the soil). Burying the crown of such a plant could kill it.

Henry Francis Du Pont covered the rolling hills of his estate at Winterthur (pictured here) with bulbs, perennials, and shrubs. Before any plant was added to this shaded landscape, it was carefully evaluated for suitability, including color compatibility and hardiness.

▼ Larger Containers

The larger the container, the more mature the plant it can hold. Large containers have become very popular, particularly for impatient gardeners who want instant flowers in their beds and borders. Because the root system is so developed in this type of container, it is extremely important to check to see if it is tangled. Gently pull the entire plant out of the container to see if the roots have circled around the inside of the pot. When the roots are this tightly bound, they will often remain in such a position even after planting, and eventually the entire plant will die. To forestall such a calamity, gently pry apart the roots before putting the plant in the hole. If this does not work, it will be necessary to cut some of the roots apart. Then plant in the same way as other potted plants.

Planting Lawns and Ground Covers

Preparation is the key to the successful installation of either lawns or wide expanses of ground covers. Follow these five steps before you begin to plant:

Test the soil with a kit from a local garden center (buy a good one), or send soil samples to your county cooperative extension office. In this way, you can learn about your soil's nutrient levels and acidity and what adjustments are necessary.

Next, eliminate weeds in the area you wish to plant by tilling the soil, by hand-pulling the weeds, or by using a postemergent herbicide.

Then, nourish the soil. Add any needed nutrients and correct, if necessary, the acidity or alkalinity (or pH) of your soil. (The pH can be altered to a modest degree, but don't plan on making major changes.)

After you've added nutrients, till the soil to work in fertilizers and other soil amendments and to loosen the soil so that the roots can easily establish themselves. If your soil has so many tree roots that it is impossible to till, you should not be growing grass in the area. Instead, plant ground covers in the soil pockets between root outcroppings.

Finally, use a garden rake to remove rocks, roots, and other debris brought to the surface by tilling and to smooth out the planting area.

▼ Planting Lawns

You can use seed, sod, or sprigs to install a new lawn. When using seed, buy the highest-quality mix recommended for your climate area and for shaded locations. Check the label to make sure the purity and germination percentages are high. The label should also specify the recommended number of pounds to sow per 1,000 square feet of lawn.

Scatter the seed evenly over the prepared soil. Lightly rake the seed into the soil, then use a roller to

Golden star (Chrysogonum virginianum) *needs moist, well-drained soil in order to spread and cover shaded areas. When given the right growing conditions, this plant produces carpets of golden yellow flowers in spring.*

firm the surface. Rolling helps germination.

Keep the newly planted surface constantly moist but not saturated. As the seeds begin to germinate, reduce the frequency but increase the amount of water. In four to six weeks, you can treat the grass seedlings as an established lawn.

Use the same watering regimen for lawns planted with sprigs. The sprigs should be evenly spread over the prepared soil and planted by hand or with special equipment. It is helpful to cover the sprigs with a thin layer of topsoil and then to roll the entire area to ensure good contact with the soil.

If you use sod, lay the strips in a bricklike pattern and make sure the edges are tightly butted against

Planting Lawns and Ground Covers CONTINUED

English ivy (Hedera helix 'Hibernica') is popular as a low-maintenance ground cover, but it can also be used as a vining plant to decorate trees and walls.

1 *Ivy is a beautiful ground cover and an excellent tree climber. To decorate trees in your shade area, first loosen the soil with a hand fork.*

2 *To ensure adequate drainage and to lessen competition with tree roots, raise the soil level and edge it with stones.*

3 *While ivy will often climb a tree when left on its own, you can get much faster and more uniform results by encircling the trunk with wire.*

4 *After the wire circle is in place, plant the ivy around the base of the tree. Firm the soil after planting and then water gently.*

5 *In a few days the ivy will settle in. Gently guide it to the wire mesh. Check every other day to make sure the ivy has taken hold.*

6 *The finished result—a fountain of lush green ivy spouting up amid a thick green carpet—is a beautiful and low-maintenance creation.*

Planting Lawns and Ground Covers CONTINUED

each other. Here again, use a roller to make sure the sod is in good contact with the soil. Unlike lawns with seeds and sprigs, those newly covered with sod must be soaked heavily every day for the first two weeks until the roots adhere firmly to the soil.

▼ Planting Ground Covers

Most ground covers are perennials and should be planted as such. Because they cover a large area, however, spacing is a key consideration. One way to space ground covers is to make a grid of 6- to 12-inch squares and to place a plant at every intersection. Another method is to use a diagonal grid and to place a plant in the center of each box in a staggered pattern.

Water each plant after it is firmly in place. Check for signs of wilting over the following week or two, and water as necessary until the plants establish themselves and begin to show new growth.

▼ Planting Moss

If the growing conditions in a shaded spot do not favor a lawn or a ground cover, moss may offer a beautiful, low-maintenance alternative.

One way to establish a large planting of moss is to transplant moss from a location where you don't want it. Dig up a clump of moss, turn it upside down, then rinse off the soil to expose the hairlike roots. Turn the clump right side up and carefully place it into muddy soil that has been cleared of all other plant material. Step gently on the patch of moss to remove air bubbles, then seal the edges with mud.

Another way to plant moss is actually a form of seeding. Dig up a clump of moss and let it dry. Crumble it up and sprinkle the moss bits over muddy soil that has been cleared. Keep the area moist until new moss starts growing.

TIMESAVING TIP

Mulch with organic matter right after planting a ground cover. The mulch will save you hours of weeding and watering by smothering weeds and conserving soil moisture.

1 Use moss as a ground cover to attain a lush green carpet in a shade setting. To create such an attraction in your garden, first dig up clumps of moss from another part of your property.

5 To ensure lush growth, rather than patchy spots, mix humus-rich soil into your planting area. Once this soil is evenly distributed, level it with a rake.

2 Cover the dug-up moss with wet newspaper to keep it damp and dark. Continue to dampen the newspaper until you are ready to plant the moss in its new location.

3 Proper site preparation for your moss garden is essential. Remove all weeds using a hand fork, as shown here, or a trowel. If necessary, sift the dirt to remove unwanted debris.

4 You need acid soil to grow moss. A pH test will let you know if your soil is suitable. If the test registers neutral or alkaline (7.0 to 9.0), acidify the planting area with sulfur.

6 Now it's time to start planting the moss turfs. Place these in quilt fashion, with each clump touching another, so that there is no room for unwanted seeds to germinate.

7 Ferns are often very attractive in a moss garden. If you like this look, plant a fern in a designated area and then continue placing moss around it.

8 Water when planting is completed. Use a watering can with a fan-head sprayer to deliver a large quantity of water gently. Water daily until plants settle in.

Planting Bulbs

*T*here are many lovely bulbs that can add color and beauty to a shade garden. Most of these need good drainage. If you plant a bulb too deep or too shallow, or in too much shade or too much light, you can easily correct the situation. If you plant a bulb in a constantly wet area, however, it usually will not live.

Once you know your site has good drainage (see page 56), planting bulbs is easy. A bulb planter with depth markings makes it even simpler. The rule of thumb is to plant two and one-half times as deep as the bulb's diameter. Thus, a 1-inch crocus would be planted 2½ inches deep. The markings on the side of the bulb planter tell you how far down you have dug.

In the past bone meal was recommended as a fertilizer for bulbs. But manufacturers now sterilize bone meal, so few nutrients are left. Chemically added nutrients are quickly released and absorbed by roots and do not supply long-term nutrition as old-fashioned, unsterilized bone meal did.

If you wish to add fertilizer, use a granular product with a 9-9-6 ratio of nitrogen, phosphorus, and potassium, and scratch it into the soil at the bottom of the planting hole. Many bulbs, such as snowdrops *(Galanthus nivalis)*, wood hyacinths *(Endymion hispanicus)*, and flowering onions *(Allium* spp.*)*, spread on their own without any fertilizer.

To add lots of color to your shade garden, plant your bulbs in layers. Plant larger, later-blooming bulbs, such as lilies, at their proper depth; then, in the next soil layer before the planting hole is completely covered, plant shallow-rooted bulbs, such as crocuses. Alternatively, overplant bulbs with impatiens, torenias, or other shallow-rooted annuals.

Tuberous begonias like to be protected from bright sun. Here, they are sheltered with an umbrella of ferns (Adiantum venustum) *and a carpet of Persian violets* (Exacum affine).

1 Because bulbs need good drainage in order to survive in a garden, it is extremely important to prepare the soil properly before planting. First, dig and clear the site.

2 Even if the soil appears loamy, it can't hurt to add leaf mold to the planting area. This helps to ensure that the soil will continue to drain well over many years.

3 After the leaf mold is thoroughly mixed in, smooth and rake the soil so that it is level. Sift out any broken roots or rocks that are in the area.

4 For an informal look, which is particularly attractive for a planting of daffodils, simply scatter the bulbs in a random arrangement on top of the prepared soil.

5 Using either a hand trowel (shown here) or a bulb planter, plant each bulb where it has landed. Sprinkle an 8-8-8 fertilizer on the soil at a rate of 1 tablespoon per square foot.

6 Once all the bulbs are planted and the soil surface is fertilized, walk over the area to firm the soil. Then, cover the soil with a layer of shredded leaf mulch. Water gently.

Planting Trees and Shrubs

EARTH·WISE TIP

Adding fertilizer to the soil mix or the planting area after installing shrubs or trees may harm, rather than help, your newly established plants. Fertilizer harms new woody plants by burning tender root tips and by stimulating rapid growth, which puts pressure on root systems to provide nutrients to the plants while adapting to new surroundings. Wait a year after planting before fertilizing trees and shrubs.

Unless you purchase very young seedlings, trees and shrubs are expensive to buy. And the more mature the plant, the higher the price. Therefore, it is particularly important to install woody plants correctly.

As discussed in the first chapter, make sure that the trees and shrubs you want will thrive in the light, drainage, climate, and soil conditions present on your property. Also, find out the plants' mature height and width and if their overall form will blend with the setting in your garden. Once installed, large shrubs and trees are difficult—and expensive—to move.

There are three basic steps in planting trees and shrubs: preparing the planting area, the actual planting, and aftercare.

▼ Preparing the Planting Area

The key to digging the planting hole, or "pit," is to make sure that the excavated area is large enough for all the shrub or tree roots to fit comfortably.

The hole must be wide enough to prevent the development of twisted roots, which ultimately will kill a plant. Nurseries use a simple formula to determine the planting hole's width: double the diameter of the spread of bare-root plants, or double the entire root ball of balled-and-burlapped plants. Make the hole 2 or 3 inches deeper than the bottom of the deepest root or the bottom of the root ball.

Remove any tree roots or rocks from the planting hole to give the roots of the new plant a chance to settle in without being crowded or blocked.

Place the soil you have removed in a container or wheelbarrow in which it can be thoroughly mixed with organic matter, such as compost, peat moss, or leaf mold. Use one part organic matter for two parts soil.

Do not add fertilizer to either the soil mix or the area after planting. The garden soil may well provide all the nutrients your plants need (a soil test will give you this information). If you do need to boost nutrient levels, you can wait until the next growing season before adding any fertilizer.

▼ Planting

The method for planting trees and shrubs varies with the kind of root packaging. In general, woody ornamentals are sold as bare-root plants, in containers, or balled and burlapped.

As with bare-root annuals and perennials (see pages 56–58), set bare-root trees or shrubs on top of a mound of soil at the bottom of the planting hole. You should form this mound from the mixture of soil and organic matter you created after digging the hole. Gently spread the roots over and down the sides of the mound, cutting and removing any that are broken or badly twisted, and make sure that the root crown is even with the soil level. With large trees and shrubs, this can be difficult, but correct planting depth is essential.

One great advantage to planting shrubs and trees sold in containers is that you can place the entire container in the hole to check the planting depth and see if you have excavated enough soil. A drawback is that plants in containers often become rootbound, or potbound, before you buy them. The roots of a potbound plant circle the inside of the container. Roots surrounding the outer edge of the root ball imprison those inside. In severe cases, the roots cannot break out of the pattern, even after the plant is planted in a properly prepared hole.

Thus, you need to carefully inspect the root structure of a plant after you remove it from a container. Gently shake loose the soil and try to separate the roots so that they can spread. If the roots are too tightly bound together, you will probably have to sever one or two to loosen the binding.

You don't need to make a mound of dirt on which to place the plant. Dig a hole about as deep as the height of the root ball and somewhat wider. Loosen the soil in the bottom and sides of the hole. Then place the plant, along with any soil that clings to the loosened roots, into the planting hole. Make sure the root crown is at soil level.

Woody ornamentals not grown in containers are dug from nursery fields in order to be sold. Once these plants are "harvested," the nursery wraps their roots—and the soil in which they were dug—in burlap. The bottom of the plant then looks like a huge ball—hence the term "balled and burlapped." This is the most common form in which large plant material is transported and sold.

These shrubs and trees arrive on your property as convalescents: they are suffering from the trauma of being dug out of a field. They should never get thirsty or lie out in hot sun before planting.

As with a container plant, carefully place a balled-and-burlapped tree or shrub into a prepared hole. Then, just snip the strings holding the burlap in place and cut away as much of the burlap as possible. The bottom of the burlap can remain in the planting hole—as long as it is really burlap. Some nurseries use imitation burlap made from plastic fibers, and this material must be completely removed, as it will not rot away underground and will confine the roots.

No matter how the roots are packaged, once the shrub or tree is in place you can fill in the hole, gently firming the soil as you go to make sure there are no air pockets. Water to settle the soil, then add more soil as needed to bring it to the correct level.

Once the soil is level with the surrounding garden area and the root crown of the plant, create a saucer to prevent excessive water runoff. Make a ridge of soil several inches out from the trunk or around the margin of the planting hole, to act as a dike and capture water for the roots and prevent runoff. Finally, spread a thin 2- to 3-inch layer of organic mulch to inhibit weed growth and keep the soil moist.

▼ Aftercare

Watering is the most important chore after you plant a new shrub or tree. Water slowly but thoroughly, as often as necessary to keep the soil from drying out. New plants need constant, even moisture, not periodic dousings. Make sure they receive adequate moisture throughout their first growing season.

Once your new shrub or tree has been planted, step back and take a critical look at it. Does it have any broken or deformed limbs? Prune these off immediately. Is its shape pleasing to you? If not, prune again to the desired effect. Also review the plant's overall nature. If it is heavily leafed out, selectively trim some of the branches to ease the transition for the roots, which need to concentrate their energy on growing in the new spot. If you transplant early in the season, before leaves have emerged, you may not need to prune at all.

Finally, if your shrub or tree is very tall, top-heavy, or in a windy spot, you probably need to stake it for its first year. Install two sturdy wooden stakes, one on either side of the trunk, and fasten the tree to them with wire. Thread the wire near the tree through a garden hose to avoid damaging the bark. Leave some play in the wire to let the tree flex in the wind: this strengthens it.

TROUBLESHOOTING TIP

When planting shrubs or trees on hills or steep slopes, carve out a small terrace for your planting hole. This allows the plants to grow straight and keeps them from toppling over.

Planting in Special Situations

Many invasive plants, such as spiderwort (Tradescantia spp.) *and lily-of-the-valley* (Convallaria majalis), *do not have room to spread rampantly when placed in soil pockets bounded by tree roots. Place fast-spreading flowers in soil pockets deep enough to cover their roots, and the plants will thrive in contained clumps rather than overrunning your woodland garden.*

*B*oth design features and the passage of time create situations that call for special planting techniques. For example, a patio in a cool, shaded location can be turned into a garden in its own right. A dry stone wall can also hold some small plants. A shade garden can serve as an outdoor home for houseplants during summer months. You may also want to plant on top of or around tree roots, especially in a woodland garden.

Small, low-maintenance, shade-loving plants can thrive in shallow nooks and crannies carefully created between the paving stones or bricks of a patio. Just make sure that the drainage is excellent. Lady's-mantle *(Alchemilla vulgaris)* and creeping polemonium *(Polemonium reptans)*, for example, provide not only colorful flowers in such a setting but also handsome foliage. The information for planting ferns in flagstones, shown in the step-by-step photographs at right and opposite, can be used in planting perennials and annuals in patio areas as well.

You can also make planting pockets in a stone wall. Where there is a sizable gap between stones, clean out the pocket and fill it with a good soil mix. Gently tuck a small plant, perhaps a fern or some edging lobelia, into the soil and water as needed.

If you want to plant in an area riddled with both tree roots and weeds, you are in luck. The presence of weeds indicates that the roots are not robbing the soil of all moisture and nutrients. Shallow-rooted plants that tend to be invasive, such as bishop's weed

1 *When planting among patio stones, choose a young plant. The roots on the fern pictured here will eventually spread below the stones and its foliage will fill out.*

(Aegopodium podagraria), are especially appropriate for such situations. Their shallow roots can survive on the thin layer of soil above the knobby tree roots, and their normally invasive habit is contained.

Before you can plant over tree roots, you must remove all the weeds. Root competition is fierce in such a setting, and you need to give your shade flowers every possible advantage. Once you have cleared the area, dig down with your trowel to see how deep the soil is. If you can reach 3 to 4 inches into the earth before hitting roots, the area should be suitable for small bulbs, such as snowdrops *(Galanthus nivalis)*, crocuses, and miniature daffodils *(Narcissus spp.)*. Because drainage is so important to the overall health and longevity of bulb plants, try to dig the hole as deep as 5 or 6 inches. Cover the bottom with sand

2 *Once you have chosen your plant and determined it is the appropriate size, dig out the planting hole. If the soil is hard, add compost or humus at this time.*

3 *Place the plant in the hole and gently press it into place. Clean off any extra dirt from the flagstones and then water thoroughly.*

to improve drainage, and then add a layer of mixed organic matter and soil to increase nutrients. Pat this down, place your bulb, and cover it with the soil you have removed.

Shallow-rooted perennials, such as Jacob's-ladder *(Polemonium* spp.)*, epimediums, and white wood aster *(A. divaricatus)*, can also be tucked in among tree roots. Dig a hole slightly larger than the root structure of the flower you are planting, add a bit of organic matter, and then place the plant in its pocket and firmly press down on the soil. Water well.

The charming but invasive sweet violet (Viola odorata) is a perfect shade flower for stone walls. It thrives in such tough but contained surroundings, and its fragrant flowers perfume spring breezes.

Planting in Special Situations CONTINUED

TIMESAVING TIP

Don't spend fruitless hours trying to plant in woodland settings when the soil is wet. The earth becomes quite compacted when overly wet and is almost impossible to work with. For easier planting, wait until the ground dries out somewhat.

Many invasive plants, such as spiderworts *(Tradescantia spp.)* and lily-of-the-valley *(Convallaria majalis)*, spread by underground root systems. When these plants are placed in soil pockets bounded by tree roots, they do not have the room to romp around. To incorporate these flowers in a woodland garden, simply make sure the soil pockets among the tree roots are deep enough to hold the flower roots, then firm the plants in place. Encased by the tree roots, new plants should grow into contained clumps rather than rampant rivers of plants.

▼ **Houseplants in the Garden**

Many houseplants enjoy the fresh air and gentle breezes outdoors after spending a winter cooped up inside. Depending on the size and attractiveness of the containers, houseplants can become an integral part of the shade garden in summer.

If the containers are not too large, you can dig holes and sink the plant, pot and all, into the ground. During the warm months, the plant will seem to grow naturally in your garden. When the weather begins to turn cool in fall, dig up the pot, clean it off, and bring the plant back into your home.

This technique is especially effective with foliage houseplants. Surround the sunken plant with colorful annuals, such as impatiens or wax begonias, for a handsome, almost instant, display.

Plants whose containers are either too large or too ornate to be placed in the ground can be used to decorate a porch, deck, patio, or other outdoor living space. Set individual plants on pedestals, or group plants on stands or shelves for a massed effect. Small plants can be placed in window boxes, with the tops of the pots camouflaged with damp sphagnum moss.

▼ **Moving Plants**

When a treasured plant has outgrown its location in terms of size or appearance, it is often possible to relocate it to another part of your property. Such movement requires care and forethought. If the loss of the plant would be particularly upsetting, hire a landscape contractor to do the transplanting.

Decide which plants need to be moved at the height of the growing season, when it is most apparent if a plant no longer belongs in its current location. Tag any plants that should be moved.

The best time for transplanting trees and shrubs is in fall, after the plant has lost its foliage but before the ground is frozen. If the plant is an evergreen, be sure to prune top growth to compensate for root loss before the move. Gardeners north of zone 5 should transplant in spring.

Prepare the new planting hole before you dig up the plant. It's helpful to have a wheelbarrow or cart available if you are moving a large plant.

Dig up the plant, taking as much soil around the roots as possible. Then carefully place the shrub or tree in its new home, and water immediately. Be sure to keep the soil evenly moist while the plant adapts to its new location.

Both indoors and out, the flask philodendron (P. martianum) needs less light than most other plants. It does not like intense heat, however, and should be situated in a cool setting when placed outdoors in summer.

Houseplants do not take kindly to the great outdoors, as they need to be protected from wind and sun. They are perfect, however, for decorating shaded corners on a patio by a house. Group them to create an instant garden.

Collecting and Saving Seeds

When collecting seeds from your favorite shade plants, only work with species plants because seeds from hybrids and cultivars do not always breed true. Also make sure the mother plant is healthy; a preexisting disease can affect both the seeds and the genes.

For many gardeners, collecting seeds to duplicate a favorite impatiens is a waste of time and effort because these flowers are almost universally hybrids, which means they will not reproduce. The only way to duplicate them exactly is to propagate the plants from cuttings (see pages 81–83).

With these caveats aside, collecting and saving seeds is relatively easy, rewarding you with a very inexpensive supply of your favorite flowers.

If possible, collect seeds when they are mature but before the seed capsules open. You can tell a capsule is about to burst by its change in color; the browner and drier it becomes, the closer it is to splitting. If you are unsure when seeds are mature, place a small paper bag or envelope over the seed capsule, tie it shut around the stem, and wait for the capsule to open; then, collect the seeds from the bag.

Now, spread your seeds out on dry newspapers in a warm, bright, well-ventilated place for several weeks. If you don't have a greenhouse (the perfect spot for drying seeds), try a sunny windowsill.

Once the seeds are thoroughly dry, clean them. Remove the seedpod and any chaff or other material attached to the seed. Then, put the seeds in a paper seed packet labeled with the plant name, flower color, and date of seed collection. Store the packet in a cool, dry, airy place not subject to frost. A refrigerator kept at a constant temperature of 35°F to 40°F is ideal. Keep the seed packet in a tightly capped glass jar.

Growing plants from seeds collected in your own garden is exciting and rewarding. To reproduce ferns in your garden, collect and sow the spores from the back of the fronds. You will always find it fascinating to witness their reproductive cycle.

1 *Money plant* (Lunaria annua) *seeds look like dark spots in the "silver dollars." Simply peel away the covering tissue and the seeds will fall out.*

2 *Because money plant seeds are dark brown, collect them on a lighter-colored surface. It is best to plant them immediately rather than to store them over winter.*

1 *Found on the back of the fronds, fern spores should be collected soon after they have ripened. They look like tiny black or brown dots when they are ripe.*

2 *Collect fern spores by gently tapping them onto a white dish, as shown here, or by drying the fern in a closed paper bag and then shaking it until the spores drop to the bottom.*

Propagating Ferns from Spores

1 Fresh fern spores germinate much better than spores that have been stored for a long time. After you collect the spores, fill a sterilized container with sterile soil mix.

2 Carefully smooth out the soil mix, as the spores are so fine they could be buried in ridges. Next, gently tap the spores onto the surface of the mix.

3 Water gently until the resulting mixture is evenly damp but not soaked. When first starting to grow your own ferns, you will have the most success with Adiantum and Pteris species.

4 To ensure constant moisture throughout the germination period, cover the dish with plastic, or a glass cover. Place the dish in a warm place out of direct sun.

5 The first tiny plants are called prothallia. Carefully transfer them into pots of moist, sterile soil. When true fronds form, plant the ferns in your garden.

Division

*D*ivision is not only a quick and effective propagation method but also a way to keep plants vigorous and healthy. You will better understand how and when to divide your shade plants after you recognize why periodic division is necessary.

The two primary reasons to divide a plant are to increase stock and to maintain health.

Division is often the cheapest way to obtain extra plants. For many shade garden flowers, however, division (or another means of vegetative propagation) is also the only way to reproduce plants at home. Many garden plants are sterile cultivars and hybrids that produce no seed or do not breed true from seed and are difficult to propagate from cuttings.

Do not let greed rule your decision to divide a plant. You must be confident that it is large enough to be divided and that in creating new plants, the shock of surgery will not be fatal for the original.

Division is an essential component in maintaining the health and vigor of many shade plants, particularly perennials and bulbs. Plant health, in turn, influences the kinds of tools used and the type of division. A dying middle and a packed plant mass are the two most common reasons for using division as a maintenance method.

Some shade flowers, such as garden phlox *(P. maculata* and *P. paniculata)*, beebalm *(Monarda didyma)*, and Jacob's-ladder *(Polemonium spp.)*, have a life cycle similar to that of the ripples formed when a stone is thrown into a pool. There is initial activity in the center; then gradually the action shifts to a receding perimeter as the ripple widens. The center of the plant becomes too thick and woody to put forth abundant foliage and flowers, and you will begin to notice a ring of foliage and flowers around an empty plant center.

Depending on the size of the plant, you can use either a trowel or a spade to cut out and throw away the tough, nonproducing inner part without digging up the entire plant. The resulting plant looks like a doughnut.

You then have two options. The first method involves lifting the entire plant from the ground and breaking its round, doughnut-shaped structure into sections. Each section should contain a minimum of two or three stems, along with some roots. Plant the individual sections in the same way the undivided plant was growing. The second option is to carefully cut a chunk of the plant, roots and all, from the outer ring and place this in the empty center, where the tough, woody part once was.

Other plants, such as coralbells *(Heuchera sanguinea)*, have fibrous roots that crawl on top of one another. Those at the bottom of the heap suffer, and those on top often lose contact with the soil. This intertwining mass of roots needs to be pulled apart. To do so, remove the whole plant with a shovel or trowel and then gently tug apart the roots or sever them cleanly with a sharp knife. Replant the divisions.

Dividing for the sake of appearance is really a way of thinning out plants. The "thinnings" can be planted elsewhere on your property, given to friends, or composted. You know it's time to divide when clumps of perennials or bulbs look overgrown or have spread out of bounds.

After several years, many hostas and other perennials form immense mounds that are just too big for their location. To divide a huge hosta, first dig up the plant. Insert two digging forks, back to back, into the center of the clump. Pressing outward on the handle of each fork, pry the plant apart. If the center of the clump is thick and woody, discard it. Depending on

Division CONTINUED

1 Hostas are shade garden gems that you can let grow into huge clumps or easily divide to create more plants. A complete division begins with digging up the entire plant.

2 The hosta shown above is small enough for you to use a trowel to divide the roots. With a very big clump, you may need a spade to make a clean division.

3 Hosta clumps consist of tightly packed individual plants. To divide them, cut apart a group of leaves with attached roots, and pull this section apart from the root mass.

4 Collect the desired number of divisions and place them in a prepared bed. This is a good time to enrich the soil with humus or compost.

5 The new hosta divisions are top-heavy with foliage. Given this condition, it is especially important to firm the soil after each planting.

6 Use a watering can with a spout up to 3 feet long. This will allow you to maneuver under the hosta foliage and to water the soil directly.

1 *Many lilies produce small bulbs, called bulbils, on the leaf axils of their stems. These generally appear as small black balls and are best collected in late summer.*

2 *Store dried bulbils over winter in dry peat. In spring, plant them in the same way as seeds in a bed or pot. Wait two to three years for flowering-size bulbs to form.*

the size of the clump, each half can then be further divided in a similar manner. Sometimes, hosta clumps are so tough and woody that it is necessary to split them with a spade rather than prying them apart with digging forks. This method works well for most large clumps of plants.

▼ When and How to Divide Plants

There are some plants—such as flowering onions (*Allium* spp.)—that are so tough and so adaptable that they can be divided at just about any time of year. Most others, however, require a bit of pampering. The best timing is determined by the reason for the division as well as the kind of plant that is being divided.

When dividing plants to increase their stock, do so in early spring. Since the plants are just starting to grow, division is not much of a shock to their systems. It is simply a matter of separating roots that have been quietly resting over winter. Plants that bloom in early spring, however, can be divided in fall to avoid interfering with their flowering.

Division for health purposes generally takes place soon after the blooming period is finished. In a shady garden, overcrowded spring perennials can be divided in midsummer, although in hotter, sunnier gardens it is better to wait until fall. Divide summer perennials in fall, and late summer and fall perennials with the first flush of growth the following spring.

Bulbs are best divided after they finish blooming and right before they go dormant. Divide daffodils, for example, in late spring or early summer, and summer bloomers, such as lilies, in the fall.

Division CONTINUED

Use the following guidelines in dividing your plants, whatever the season or reason.

▼ Divide plants on a day that is refreshing not only to the gardener but also to the plants. Cool, sunny days are fine, but cool, overcast days are best. When you don't have the luxury of waiting for the right weather in which to divide your shade flowers, try to do the job in late afternoon or early evening. That way, they'll have the relative coolness of the evening to help them adjust to their surgery.

▼ Prepare a new home for your divided plants. Look for an appropriately sized new space, and prepare the soil in that area. Dig a hole about twice the depth and diameter of each plant's roots. Check the quality of the soil with regard to drainage; if necessary, add peat moss, sand, or other soil conditioners.

▼ Try to leave some of the plant in its home base, to serve as a future source of the plant in case the divisions die.

▼ Check the root structure of the plant being divided, and then plant the separated parts similarly. The roots of coralbells *(Heuchera* spp.*)*, for example, are very shallow and spread out just under a top layer of soil.

▼ Be sure to water thoroughly after each division is planted, and continue to water regularly for at least a week or until the plant appears to be settling in and foliage growth resumes.

▼ Use care in selecting any fertilizer to add. All commercial fertilizers come with three numbers on their packaging. When incorporating fertilizer in the soil for newly divided plants, choose a nitrogen-free formula (the first number on the fertilizer bag should be 0). Nitrogen promotes vegetative growth, and for newly divided plants root growth is the top priority.

One reason to explore propagating the beautiful, shade-tolerant Canada lily (Lilium canadense) *on your own is that it is an expensive plant to buy.*

▼ If you divide plants shortly after they finish blooming, the plants are equipped with abundant foliage. Give each division a "crew cut" so that all leaves are only 1 or 2 inches long. This allows a plant to acclimate itself to a new setting without having to concentrate on foliage maintenance.

1 Lilies are usually propagated through a form of division using scales that look like garlic cloves. First, dig up the entire bulb in early fall after the lily has flowered.

2 Carefully remove a few scales from the bulb. These scales should be separated as close to the base of the bulb as possible.

3 Insert the scales into a mix of equal parts peat moss and sand. Water sparingly at first so that the scales do not rot. After roots appear, increase the amount of water.

4 Replant the mother bulb as soon as its scales are removed. Only the mother bulb will give you flowers during the few years seeds take to reach flowering size.

1 *Creeping phlox (P. stolonifera) lives up to its common name by sending out shoots (called stolons) that root as they wander. To divide this plant, first locate rooted stolons.*

2 *Next, with sharp garden scissors or pruners, sever the link between the rooted stolon and the mother plant. Carefully dig up the now-isolated rooted stolon.*

3 *Immediately replant each stolon division elsewhere in the garden. Or put all divisions in a specially prepared tray, as shown here, and replant them at the same time. Water thoroughly.*

Creeping phlox (P. stolonifera), which graces spring shade settings with carpets of colorful flowers, is an exceptionally easy plant to divide. See the step-by-step photos above for more details.

Cuttings

Propagating a plant from cuttings involves severing part of the plant and encouraging the severed part to form roots and grow into a new plant that looks exactly like the parent.

There are two basic sources of cuttings: a plant's tip or stem and its roots. How cuttings are handled depends on which part of the plant you are using.

▼ Tip and Stem Cuttings

The only difference between a tip and a stem cutting is that the former, as its name implies, comes from the end of a stem and the latter can comprise any part of a stem. Indeed, you can cut one stem into many pieces and root each piece.

Whether you take one or more cuttings from a stem, be sure each is sliced just below a point called a node. This is the point where a leaf joins the stem. You must have at least one node on a stem—but can have more if you wish—in order for it to take root.

Remove all the leaves from the bottom third of the cutting. Many gardeners then like to dip the bottom of the stem into a hormone rooting powder to increase the chances of success; others feel this is unnecessary or varies with the particular perennial or shrub being rooted. In any case, dipped or not, the cleaned stem is placed in a container of moist rooting medium, with the node just above the soil line. One good rooting medium combines equal parts of peat moss and sharp builder's sand.

Keep the medium evenly moist while the cuttings root. You can cover the container with plastic and place it in a propagation chamber (a clear, closed container like a terrarium), or you can check the cuttings periodically and water if the medium feels dry.

Cuttings need light, but not hot sun. Place them under plant lights indoors or outside in very bright,

open shade. Avoid sunny windowsills, especially if you are using a propagation chamber; or the cuttings may cook on a sunny day.

Shade trees or shrubs that are frequently grown from cuttings include hydrangeas, hollies *(Ilex* spp.*)*, and magnolias. Popular ground covers and vines that are easily propagated from cuttings include ivy *(Hedera* spp.*)*, spotted dead nettle *(Lamium maculatum)*, honeysuckle *(Lonicera* spp.*)*, and periwinkle *(Vinca* spp.*)*. The step-by-step photos on page 83 show how easy it is to propagate pachysandra from stem cuttings.

Hardy geranium species (*G. himalayense,* and others), coralbell *(Heuchera* spp.*)*, and cardinal flower *(Lobelia cardinalis)* are among the many shade-tolerant perennials that are easily and inexpensively propagated by cuttings.

Perhaps easiest of all are two popular annuals: wax begonias and impatiens. Begonias, especially, come in so many different colors and shades—and so rarely breed true—that propagation by cuttings is the best way to save a plant you particularly like.

▼ Root Cuttings

Propagation from root cuttings is a bit trickier than from tip or stem cuttings and should be used only when other methods are not practical. Three shade flowers that are readily propagated by root cuttings are bear's-breech *(Acanthus mollis)*, leadwort *(Ceratostigma plumbaginoides)*, and common bleeding-heart *(Dicentra spectabilis)*. Bleeding-heart rarely sets seed, and even when it does, the seeds are very difficult to germinate.

When propagating by root cuttings, first lift the dormant plant out of the ground. Snip off a 3- to 4-inch section of a sturdy, healthy root. Make the cut

Cuttings CONTINUED

Periwinkle (Vinca minor) *has been a popular evergreen ground cover in American gardens since colonial times. Though it can be increased by division, you can obtain many more plants by rooting cuttings.*

nearest the crown of the plant a straight one; make the cut at the outermost area of the root on a slant so that you will remember which end is the top of the cutting and which is the bottom.

Place the cut root vertically in a container. Make sure the flat-cut end is at the top. Fill the container to the top of the root tip with a moist, well-drained rooting medium, such as the mix of peat moss and sand recommended for tip and stem cuttings. There should be an extra inch or more at the bottom of the container to give the root tip room to spread. Cover the top of the root tip with a thin layer of sand or vermiculite no more than ½ inch deep. Lastly, replant the parent plant.

Root cuttings do best in cool surroundings, so they should not be taken at the height of summer. Depending on the perennial you are propagating, early spring or late summer into fall is the best time. For example, since the common bleeding-heart goes dormant after spring bloom, its root cuttings should be taken at the end of the garden season.

After potting up the root cuttings, place them in a cold frame or an unheated greenhouse. While keeping direct light to a minimum, try to ensure there is lots of bright, indirect light.

As with other forms of propagation, it is necessary to keep the root tip moist but not saturated. Do this by periodically checking the soil for moisture and watering as needed.

1 Pachysandra can be increased by either division or cuttings. If you opt for cuttings, take them at the end of summer or in early fall.

2 Using a clean tool, cut a 5- to 6-inch piece of healthy stem. Make the cut right below a node or leaf joint, then strip all the lower leaves.

3 Clean each cut stem. Although most stem cuttings need to be rooted in a moist mixture of peat and sand, pachysandra will root in water.

4 One great advantage of rooting cuttings in water is that you can easily see how fast roots are developing. These cuttings are ready to be transplanted.

5 When planting rooted cuttings, make sure that the soil is properly prepared. These plants have been growing only in water and will need a loamy soil.

6 After all the rooted cuttings are in place, water thoroughly but gently. Keep the ground evenly moist until the plants start to produce new growth and spread.

CHAPTER 4

Maintaining Shade Gardens

a shade garden will offer you a fair amount of leeway if you choose plants that are suited to your soil and climate conditions. The absence of glaring light means mistakes and untidiness are not as readily apparent as they are in sunnier settings. • Over time, some simple maintenance chores will ensure the continued attractiveness of your garden and also the health of your plants. • This chapter reviews what you must do to care for your garden. Shade gardens, for the most part, require a minimal amount of care. As with any garden, you'll want to make sure your garden is properly mulched, and that your plants are properly watered, pruned, and maintained. This chapter also provides tips on keeping your garden free of pests and diseases to ensure that your shade garden will remain healthy and vigorous all season.

Care During the Season

With a well-planned design and carefully chosen plants that do not demand a lot of pampering, your garden maintenance will be minimal. The three major tasks involved in caring for a shade garden—fertilizing, mulching, and watering—are common to all kinds of gardens.

▼ Fertilizing

If you have a woodland shade garden, the soil already present probably provides all the nutrients your plants need, so you don't need to fertilize. Simply let the falling leaves and decaying organic matter in your woods enrich your garden soil just as they do in nature. If your leaves are big ones, such as those cast off by maples and oaks, you can give nature a helping hand by raking the dried leaves remaining in spring, shredding them with a shredder or power lawn mower, and then returning them to your garden beds as a mulch.

If your garden is shaded by buildings (which obviously contribute no organic matter), you should probably add compost, leaf mold, or other organic matter as a topdressing to the soil once a year, preferably in spring. One inexpensive source of organic matter is the composted leaf mulch that many municipalities offer free of charge.

Many gardeners will find the above natural fertilizer routine very satisfactory. Others, however, may wish to give an extra boost to the shade garden by enriching the soil. If you plan to grow lots of annuals and other fast-growing flowers, add a slow-release, balanced fertilizer to your beds in spring. The extra nutrients will help your plants produce larger and more colorful blossoms.

A slow-release fertilizer is best because it gives your plants food over a long period of time rather than gorging them with one large feeding. A balanced fertilizer contains equal parts of nitrogen, phosphorus, and potassium as is indicated by the same number appearing three times in a row on the fertilizer bag (e.g., 10-10-10 or 20-20-20). Balanced fertilizers come in both synthetic and organic forms. Instead of a complete fertilizer, you can add individual sources of organic nutrients, such as rock phosphate to supply phosphorus and composted livestock manure for nitrogen. Follow the package directions regarding application rates, and allow extra time for organic materials to break down and make their nutrients available to plants.

One of the very best, and unfortunately most expensive, fertilizers is liquid seaweed. This can be diluted and applied directly to plant foliage without damage; other fertilizers often cause ugly leaf burn. Liquid seaweed is a good source of trace minerals.

▼ Mulching

Mulches serve two important purposes: they conserve soil moisture and they smother weeds. An organic mulch offers an extra benefit: it adds organic matter to the soil as it decomposes.

In shade gardens, several popular plants can serve as living mulches when planted in masses. The large, lustrous leaves of many hostas, for example, effectively shade out weeds that try to emerge underneath them, and they also help keep soil moisture from evaporating. Ground covers, as their name implies, leave little room for unwanted plants and also help keep the soil moist. These two kinds of plants are staples in low-maintenance shade gardens.

In woodland gardens, fallen leaves provide an automatic mulch for the plants if you don't clean them up. If a layer of old leaves is too messy for your taste, rake the leaves up and spread a neat layer of shredded leaves, leaf mold, compost, or wood chips as a mulch. If you choose wood chips, add a nitrogen fertilizer to the soil at the end of the season to compensate for nitrogen used by the wood chips as they decompose.

▼ Watering

If your shade garden is properly mulched, you should rarely have to water. If drought is endemic to your growing area, make sure you choose plants that can tolerate dry shade, such as common columbine *(Aquilegia canadensis)*, big-root cranesbill *(Geranium macrorrhizum)*, bishop's hat *(Epimedium* spp.*)*, Lenten rose *(Helleborus orientalis)*, and lilyturf *(Liriope* spp.*)*.

If you have an unexpected dry spell, water your garden deeply at least once a week, early in the morning. Make sure the water soaks in below the covering of mulch or any ground covers.

▼ Other Tasks

Unless your garden is located in an urban area where no further construction occurs, the light in your borders will change over the years. Trees get taller or fall down, and new buildings are put up. During each garden season, watch for any significant changes in the light pattern that could affect the health of your plants and, as a result, the beauty of your setting. Where shade becomes too dense, for example, you might need to remove some limbs of trees or to add bright reflectors to garden paths, as described on pages 40–41, to get more light into the garden.

Volunteer, or self-sown, tree seedlings—maples and oaks are particularly notorious offenders—are also the bane of many shade gardeners. Keep an eye out for these unwanted plants; they are much easier to remove as tiny seedlings than as saplings.

Finally, as with any garden, begin and end your garden year with a thorough cleanup, emphasizing weeding and clearing out plant debris.

E A R T H • W I S E
T I P

During the summer months, inspect your plants for disease or insect invasions and promptly remove any affected material. In addition to making your garden more attractive, prompt removal of damaged leaves and shoots cuts down on future cleanup chores by providing less opportunity for fungal and viral diseases to settle in and spread.

The beautiful native oakleaf hydrangea (H. quercifolia) *is crowned with gorgeous flowers in summer. At the end of the garden year, its foliage turns elegant shades of red.*

Controlling Pests

Deer-Resistant Plants

If deer are hungry enough they will eat practically anything, but gardeners across the country report that deer do not like the following plants (see the encyclopedia, pages 96–126, for detailed descriptions): monkshood (Aconitum spp.), baneberry (Actaea spp.), flowering onion (Allium spp.), lily-of-the-valley (Convallaria majalis), foxglove (Digitalis spp.), and daffodil (Narcissus spp.). They also tend to avoid prickly, spiny plants.

*E*very kind of garden has its share of pests. The most common pests in a shade garden are slugs, snails, root weevils, and deer.

Although it is difficult to give them any credit at all, slugs and snails actually serve a useful function. They are part of the process of decay, in which plant material is reprocessed into soil. If only they would limit their appetites to dead leaves, millions of shade gardeners would be much happier!

These creatures need coolness and moisture, the very attributes so prevalent in shade gardens. They also adore hostas. If you are averse to using chemical baits, you may be unable to grow hostas in areas with high slug and snail populations. Even with liberal doses of poison you will probably be unable to eradicate these prolific creatures. All you can hope for is to keep them under control.

Digitalis purpurea, *commonly called foxglove, is the source for the heart drug digitalis. Because its leaves contain such a potent medicine, deer have learned to leave the plant alone.*

To deal with slugs and snails naturally, take advantage of their definite tastes in food by selecting plants they do not like to chew (see the sidebar on page 89). Also, lay down a barrier mulch of fresh-cut wood chips; the creatures will go out of their way to avoid the tannin in fresh wood. Snails, in particular, stay away from plantings protected by edgings of fresh redwood chips.

The old belief that beer will attract and drown slugs is only partially correct. Some slugs will drown in the bowl of beer you leave out, but more slugs will probably be attracted to the area than are killed, increasing your slug population. At least place the beer traps outside the garden area to draw slugs away from your flowers.

If you can, coax some toads or frogs into your garden. They thrive in the same conditions as slugs and love to eat them. To make your garden more hospitable to these slug vacuum cleaners, install a shallow dish or pan, kept constantly filled with water, in a quiet spot protected by overhanging leaves.

If these strategies do not work, try poison bait or spread diatomaceous earth (a white powder created by grinding the fossilized skeletons of tiny sea creatures) in infested areas. The poisons kill the pests, and the abrasive diatomaceous earth literally slashes them to death. Both these deterrents wash away in rain, however, and need to be reapplied.

Root weevils are also a plague in shade gardens. There are several different kinds of small dark beetles that are commonly called root weevils. All nibble the edges of the leaves of prized shade plants, such as rhododendrons, at night, and then hide during the day. Underground, their numerous offspring—appearing as soft, white larvae—feed on roots and do even more serious damage.

1 *Slugs cannot take dry heat—which is one reason they like shade gardens. Remove them from areas, such as under a slate, where they might nest.*

2 *Slugs can also be destroyed by handpicking them off plants (wear gloves!) and dropping them into a jar of soapy or salty water.*

Slug-Resistant Plants
In general, slugs do not like to chew on the following plants (see the encyclopedia, pages 96–126, for detailed descriptions): Astilbe *spp.,* hardy begonia *(B. grandis),* wild bleeding-heart *(Dicentra eximia),* foxglove *(Digitalis spp.),* Epimedium *spp.,* Lenten rose *(Helleborus orientalis),* impatiens cultivars, *and Jacob's-ladder* (Polemonium caeruleum).

These insects are extremely tough. Despite all the powerful chemicals created to kill them, root weevils live on. They are particularly fond of tender young plants. If these pests infest your garden, you should buy larger, more mature plants, which have a better chance of surviving.

Root weevils are a particular problem in new shade gardens, where their natural predators have not yet settled in. If your new plants are being seriously harmed by these pests, you may have to use poisons. Recent research suggests that the easiest and least expensive method is to thoroughly spray affected plants just once in mid-July.

Finally, deer are a major garden problem in some locations. In the absence of natural predators and with the availability of delectable garden plants, deer herds have grown tremendously. The only real guarantee against deer damage is a high (8 feet or more), sturdy fence that the animals cannot jump over. One other generally effective alternative is to grow plants that are distasteful to deer (see the sidebar on page 88); the animals have learned to avoid them.

One nice aspect of shade gardens is that they do not usually attract aphids, mites, or caterpillars. These insects prefer sunny locations. To further reduce the possibility that these pests will appear in your garden, you can apply a horticultural oil spray (also called dormant oil) to your shrubs and trees at the end of winter, right before new growth starts. Widely available at garden centers, these specially formulated oils are harmless to plants and smother the overwintering egg masses of pests. Lighter sprays have been developed that can be applied to trees and shrubs in summer as well.

Pinching and Pruning

*T*he terms "pinching" and "pruning" are used to describe the selective cutting of stems and branches. In general, pinching is applied to flowering annuals and perennials, and pruning is undertaken on shrubs and trees. Pinching promotes bushier growth and increases flower production, and pruning creates more attractive shapes, controls the direction of growth, and maintains health.

If you prefer a low-maintenance approach to shade gardening, you can skip the information on pinching and start on the pruning discussion below. Pinching is not an essential chore; indeed, for many shade plants with flowers on single spikes—plants such as monkshoods *(Aconitum* spp.*)*, astilbes, and hostas—it is forbidden: lopping off the spike would destroy the main flowering.

Other shade lovers, however, such as the annual coleus and the perennial celandine poppy *(Stylophorum diphyllum)*, respond well to pinching. Pinch off stems bearing seedpods or small flowers, back to the set of leaves below the uppermost set (see the photos below). This is a simple task, easily accomplished during a stroll through the garden.

For still other shade plants, such as foxgloves *(Digitalis* spp.*)* and perennial lobelias, pinching (or, if the stem is particularly sturdy, cutting) off the flowering spike after bloom encourages the production of flowering side shoots and considerably lengthens the bloom period.

It's your decision whether or not you want to pinch. If you notice plants getting leggy and unattractive, try cutting back the ungainly stems to make a neater-looking plant. If the plants look fine, leave

1 *Many annuals, such as the coleus pictured here, fade away after they have produced seed. Keep them alive and colorful by pinching off all flowering stems.*

2 *After you spot the first flower, check the plant two or three times a week to thwart seed production. Such minimal effort results in a lovely foliage plant.*

When grown in a naturalized woodland setting, as shown here, azaleas do not need to be pruned. In a smaller, more formal garden, however, they can be trimmed to control both size and shape.

them alone. Finally, if you want to experiment to see if a bloom period can be extended, selectively pinch back stems to see if new flowers result.

Trees and shrubs are not only larger but also more expensive than annuals and perennials. You have a financial as well as an aesthetic stake in keeping them attractive and in good health.

A tree generally needs to be pruned only if it has dead or diseased branches or if it has outgrown the allotted space. Working with these large plants requires knowledge of the kind of tree being cut as well as special equipment. It is always best to consult a professional when your trees need to be trimmed to any substantial degree. Since trees are most easily trimmed when they are dormant in late winter, make any arrangements with a tree surgeon then.

Pinching and Pruning CONTINUED

Some shrubs almost never need to be pruned. Conifers, for example, generally should not be trimmed, as many do not put forth new growth where they have been cut. Rhododendrons can be left on their own, just as the native ones in woodlands across the country are. Oakleaf hydrangea *(H. quercifolia)*, sweetspire *(Itea virginica)*, and mountain laurel *(Kalmia latifolia)* are three more native shrubs that do not usually need trimming.

However, there are occasions when even these shrubs may need pruning. After a severe winter, for example, you may need to remove dead, broken, or diseased branches. As soon as possible, cut back these branches to green, healthy wood. Bag and immediately discard all cut branches; do not chip and compost diseased wood.

If a shrub becomes leggy, you can employ a simple technique, sometimes called the "one-in-three" approach, to make it fuller and more compact. After you have grown the shrub for at least three years, prune one-third of the oldest wood each year. Cut back the old stems to just above ground level and no more than 6 inches high.

Some shrubs, such as hardy fuchsia, may suffer winterkill, which causes branches to die; others, such as rhododendrons, may eventually become too big and ungainly for their location, especially in a small garden. In both cases the shrubs can be cut back to just above ground level—no more than 6 inches high. With the rhododendron, you may have to wait several years for flowering to recur, but you will have a much neater plant that fits nicely into your garden.

The timing of pruning activities is crucial. The best rule of thumb is to prune spring-blooming shrubs right after they have flowered (usually late spring) and summer- and fall-blooming shrubs long before they flower (usually early spring).

The rationale behind this strategy is that spring-blooming shrubs, such as white forsythia *(Abelio-phyllum distichum)*, flower on wood that grew the previous year. When you trim these shrubs immediately after the last petal falls, you are cutting back old wood. If you wait until summer, you are cutting back new growth that will produce the following season's flowers. Although you will not harm this kind of shrub if you prune it in summer, you will sacrifice next year's blooms.

Shrubs that flower later in the season do so on new wood. Thus, if you prune these plants in early spring, you are cutting back the old wood that would never bear blossoms. Beautyberry *(Callicarpa* spp.), for example, flowers and bears its attractive purple fruit on new wood. If you wish to improve the shape of this attractive shrub, trim it in early spring.

In every case, make sure that the edges of your pruning tools are sharp and clean. This ensures good cuts and guards against the spread of disease.

End-of-Season and Winter Care

*I*n winter, as the shade garden year draws to a close in most parts of the country, there are several important tasks to be performed. If your broad-leaved evergreens are planted among deciduous trees or shrubs, they may have to be protected from winter winds howling through bare branches. Make a burlap shelter on the side facing into the prevailing winter winds.

If you have planted tender bulbs, such as caladiums and tuberous begonias, you may wish to save them for replanting the following season. To do so, stop watering the plants about one month before you expect the first frost. When the leaves turn yellow, lift each plant along with any soil attached to the bulb and its roots. Move the entire clump to an airy spot out of direct sun, and let it dry out. If the weather is warm, let it dry outdoors; if cold, dry indoors. When the surface of the clump is dry, trim the foliage, shake off the excess soil, and store the bulbs in a cool, dry place in paper bags. Label the bags with the type of bulb and flower color.

After the first light frosts strike and the soil begins to freeze, cover any plants that are marginally hardy with a mulch—such as shredded leaves, pine needles, or licorice roots—to form a 2- to 3-inch protective blanket. This is an especially important task in areas with minimal snow cover. Winter mulches prevent the soil from alternately thawing and refreezing during spells of mild weather, which could cause roots to heave out of the ground.

While covering up some parts of your garden, remember to expose other areas, where early bulbs, such as snowdrops and winter aconites, are planted. This gives these bulbs a chance to start the garden year extra early.

1 *Try to dig up begonia tubers before frost strikes. To overwinter these lovely plants, cut the foliage to the ground, pot the tuber, and leave it in a cool, dry area.*

2 *Once a heavy frost has turned impatiens into mush, it is time to clean up the garden. Remove weeds, diseased plants, and debris.*

Regional Calendar of Shade Garden Care

 Spring

☀ *Summer*

COOL CLIMATES

Spring

- To control pests, apply dormant oil spray on deciduous trees and shrubs when the temperature reaches 40°F for a 24-hour period. This must be done before the tree's growth starts.

- Place flower seedlings grown indoors in a protected spot outdoors to harden off for seven to ten days before planting.

- Early spring is a good time to plant and transplant shrubs. Begin as soon as the soil has thawed and dried and is ready to work.

- Separate crowded spring bulbs after they have finished flowering. Transplant extras, complete with ripening foliage, to other parts of your property.

- Set up stakes or hoops for tall perennials, such as bugbane *(Cimicifuga* spp.*)* or foxglove *(Digitalis* spp.*)* before the plants reach 1 foot high.

- Rake any remaining dead leaves and other garden debris from beds, and spread an organic mulch when plants are several inches high.

Summer

- Complete transplanting bulbs while you can still locate them, before their foliage fades.

- Plant annual impatiens and begonias to fill in bare spots left by now-dormant spring bulbs and some early perennials.

- Mow lawn to an optimal height of 2 inches. Leave the clippings in the lawn as an organic additive.

- Mulch open spaces in flower gardens with organic materials to smother annual weeds, conserve moisture, and enrich the soil.

- If aphids, mealybugs, or whiteflies are a problem, apply insecticidal soap spray on overcast, still days.

- Check for any diseased or storm-damaged branches or foliage on trees and shrubs, and promptly remove.

- On really hot days, pick a cool spot and sit back to enjoy the beauty of your garden.

WARM CLIMATES

Spring

- Consider installing a soaker hose or drip-irrigation system for watering your garden.

- Rake any remaining dead leaves and other garden debris from beds, and spread an organic mulch when plants are several inches high.

- Trim overgrown shrubs to improve their appearance just before active growth starts.

- Separate crowded spring bulbs after they have finished flowering. Transplant extras, complete with ripening foliage, to other parts of your property.

- To increase next year's flower production on azaleas, camellias, and rhododendrons, deadhead this year's blossoms once they have faded.

- Apply any needed fertilizer to container plants that have overwintered outdoors.

Summer

- Be vigilant in regularly watering spring-flowering trees and shrubs that can become stressed in dry summer heat.

- Mow lawn to an optimal height of 2 inches. Leave the clippings in the lawn as an organic additive.

- Replace mulches when they become thin. If aphids, mealybugs, or whiteflies break out, apply insecticidal soap spray on infested plants on overcast, still days.

- Check container plants to see if they need to be moved to shadier locations and to make sure they are being adequately watered.

- Check for any diseased or storm-damaged branches or foliage on trees and shrubs, and promptly remove.

- On really hot days, pick a cool spot and sit back to enjoy the beauty of your garden.

Fall

- Test the soil in all areas of the garden where you have had trouble. Contact your county cooperative extension agent for information on how to correct problems.

- Check end-of-season sales at local garden centers. Carefully examine plants before you buy them.

- Clean the garden. Compost healthy plant cuttings, but discard all diseased material.

- Plant bulbs. Early-blooming species tulips, such as *Tulipa tarda*, will often come back every year in well-drained areas around deciduous trees.

- When the soil starts to freeze, mulch in areas without snow covers. The winter mulch helps maintain soil moisture and prevents rapid soil temperature fluctuations, which can damage roots.

- When using dry autumn leaves as a mulch, keep them in place with a covering of chicken wire.

- Thoroughly clean and dry all garden tools before putting them away for the season.

- Plant pansies *(Viola × wittrockiana)* for color throughout the winter months.

- Divide and transplant spring-blooming perennials.

- Constantly clean the garden of spent or faded plants. Compost healthy plant cuttings, but discard all diseased material.

- Test the soil in all areas of the garden where you have had trouble. Contact your county cooperative extension agent for information on how to correct problems.

- Ornamental kale *(Brassica × oleracea)* flourishes at this time of year. Place pots in dark, drab spaces that need an end-of-the-year pickup.

 Winter

- Visit nearby flower shows; learn about new, low-maintenance plants by reading mail-order nursery catalogues; and search for good books to add to your garden library.

- Start plants from seed indoors. This is the cheapest, and often the only, way to obtain plants.

- Avoid using salt on icy sidewalks or driveways near your garden beds and borders. The salt will leach into your soil and damage or even destroy your plants.

- Remove heavy snow from evergreen trees and shrubs to protect branches from breaking. Allow ice to melt by itself.

- Examine the garden in late winter to see if the addition of an early-flowering shade shrub, such as witch hazel *(Hamameli* spp.*)*, would add color to a bleak winter setting.

- Gradually remove winter mulch from garden beds after night temperatures remain above 30°F.

- Take advantage of dreary days to pursue your garden education. Visit nearby flower shows; learn about new, low-maintenance plants by reading mail-order nursery catalogues; and search for good books to add to your garden library.

- In February apply nontoxic dormant oil spray to deciduous trees and shrubs when the temperature goes above 40°F for 24 hours. This reduces scale and other insects.

- Early March is a good time to prune and plant bare-root shade trees.

- Check evergreen shrubs and trees for overwintering egg masses of insect pests, and promptly remove them.

- Pick early-blooming flowers to enjoy their color and fragrance indoors.

- Thoroughly clean and dry all garden tools set aside during this season.

This table offers a basic outline of garden care by season. The tasks for each season differ for warm and cool climates: warm climates correspond to USDA Plant Hardiness zones 8 through 11, and cool climates to zones 2 through 7. Obviously, there are substantial climate differences within these broad regions. To understand the specific growing conditions in your area, consult the Zone Map on page 127. Also be sure to study local factors affecting the microclimate of your garden, such as elevation and proximity of water.

Plants for American Shade Gardens

This section provides concise information on more than 150 plants recommended for shade gardens. The plants have been selected on the basis of beauty, adaptability, and availability. A few have been included for the shade they provide, not because they tolerate or thrive in shade. To find a plant of a certain height or with flowers of a specific color—check the Growth Habit and Flower Color columns. If you need plants for a dry or moist spot, look under Growing Conditions. Or study the photos, read the descriptions, and then decide which plants will grow well in your garden.

▼ About Plant Names

Plants appear in alphabetical order by the genus name, shown in bold type. On the next line is the most widely used common name. The third listing gives the complete botanical name: genus, species, and where applicable, a variety or cultivar name.

Common names vary, but botanical names are the same everywhere. If you learn botanical names, you'll always get the plant you want from a mail-order nursery or local garden center. One gardener's white forsythia may be another gardener's Korean forsythia, but both gardeners will recognize the plant if they know its scientific name: *Abeliophyllum distichum*.

When several species in a genus are similar in appearance and cultural needs, they are listed together in a single entry in the chart. In the case of a genus containing two or more vastly different species that cannot be covered in a single entry, each of the recommended species is given a separate entry.

The second column of the chart provides a brief plant description. Look here to see if the plant is an annual or perennial, a tree or shrub, or herbaceous, and if its form is vertical, bushy, low, or vining.

▼ Flower Color

The color dots following each description indicate the color *family*; they are not a literal rendering of the flower color. A plant given a pink dot might be pale blush pink, clear pink, or bright rose pink. You will find color dots even when a plant's flowers are not mentioned in the description, as with the entries for maple trees *(Acer spp.)* on page 97.

▼ Time of Bloom

Bloom time is given by season and may vary from one region to another according to climate, weather, and growing conditions. For example, witch hazel *(Hamamelis × intermedia)* blooms in early spring in northern gardens but in late winter in warmer areas. During a cold year when spring comes late, tender plants, such as tuberous begonias, should go into the garden later and will, therefore, bloom later.

▼ Hardiness

Plant hardiness is generally an indication of the coldest temperatures a plant is likely to survive. But many plants also have limits to the amount of heat they can tolerate. In this chart hardiness is expressed as a range from the coolest to the warmest zones where the plant generally thrives. The zones are based on the newest version of the USDA Plant Hardiness Zone Map, shown on page 127.

▼ Growing Conditions

The last column summarizes the best growing conditions for the plant, including its light, moisture, and soil requirements.

		Flower Color	Time of Bloom	Growth Habit	Hardiness Zones	Growing Conditions
ABELIO-PHYLLUM KOREAN FORSYTHIA, WHITE FORSYTHIA *Abeliophyllum distichum*	A deciduous shrub (not a true forsythia) whose clusters of fragrant, 4-petaled, pink-tinged, white flowers emerge before its pairs of oval, 2- to 3-in. leaves. *A. distichum* works well as a shrub border or a backdrop for spring bulbs.	○	*Early spring*	Height: 3–5' Spread: 3–5'	5 to 8	*Full sun to light shade. Moist, well-drained, humus-rich soil. Prune after flowering to encourage a more compact form. Korean forsythia is a slow-growing shrub that becomes bushier with age.*
ACANTHUS ARTIST'S ACANTHUS, BEAR'S-BREECH *Acanthus mollis*	A semievergreen perennial with glossy, deep green, spiny, 1- to 2-ft.-long leaves and bold, 2- to 4-ft.-long spikes of white or purple-blue tubular flowers. Each flower is surrounded by a spine-tipped, pinkish purple bract.	○ ●	*Midsummer to late summer*	Height: 2–4' Spread: 3–4'	6 to 10	*Full sun to partial shade, with some afternoon shade in zones 8–10. Well-drained soil; will not tolerate soggy conditions. Mulch in winter north of zone 7. Propagate from seed in spring, or divide rootstocks in fall. Give plenty of space.*
ACER PAPERBARK MAPLE *Acer griseum*	A deciduous shrub or tree that, unlike most maples, has compound leaves of 3 small leaflets. Some cultivars turn brilliant colors in autumn. The cinnamon brown bark peels freely with age.		*Spring*	Height: 20–30' Spread: 10–30'	5 to 8	*Full sun to partial shade. Well-drained, humus-rich soil with ample moisture throughout the season.*
ACER JAPANESE MAPLE *Acer palmatum*	A deciduous shrub or small tree with a rounded crown of the palmately veined leaves typical of maples. Cultivars often have red leaves with 5 to 11 deeply dissected lobes. Japanese maple is an ideal specimen tree if space is limited.	●	*Spring*	Height: 10–25' Spread: 10–28'	5 to 9	*Full sun to partial shade. Well-drained, humus-rich soil with ample moisture throughout the season.*
ACONITUM MONKSHOOD, WOLFSBANE ◀ *Aconitum carmichaelii* *A. napellus*	Perennials bearing spikes of helmet-shaped, dark blue-violet or white flowers on tall stems with decorative, dark green, deeply lobed leaves. The roots and other parts are poisonous. Monkshood is an ideal plant for a semishady border.	○ ● ●	*A. carm.* Late summer to mid-autumn *A. nap.* Early to midsummer	*A. carm.* Height: 3–6' Spread: 1–2' *A. nap.* Height: 3–4' Spread: 1–2'	4 to 8	*Full sun to partial shade. Deep, rich, moist, well-drained soil. Monkshood grows best in cool climates. Divide plants every several years after they have reached maturity.*

◀ Indicates species shown

Plants for American Shade Gardens

		Flower Color	Time of Bloom	Growth Habit	Hardiness Zones	Growing Conditions
ACTAEA WHITE BANEBERRY ◄ *Actaea pachypoda* RED BANEBERRY *A. rubra*	Perennial plants with cylindrical clusters of thin-petaled white flowers and deep green compound leaves with toothed leaflets. A. pachypoda has white berries on pink stalks; A. rubra has red ones on green stalks. The berries are poisonous.	○	Mid-spring	Height: 1–2½' Spread: 1–2'	3 to 7	Partial to full shade. Moist, well-drained, humus-rich soil. Baneberry is an eastern native that does well in woodland conditions. It needs constant moisture but dislikes very wet soil. Divide roots in spring.
ADIANTUM SOUTHERN MAIDEN-HAIR FERN *Adiantum capillus-veneris* MAIDENHAIR FERN ◄ *A. pedatum*	Graceful, delicate, hardy native ferns with fan-shaped fronds borne on wiry, dark stems arising from rhizomes that spread slowly underground. The spores are clustered on the undersides of the leaflets.		No flowers	Height: 8–18" Spread: 6–12"	A. cap. 8 to 10 A. ped. 2 to 8	Partial to full shade. Moist, humus-rich soil. Southern maidenhair can be grown indoors as a container plant in colder climates.
AJUGA BUGLEWEED ◄ *Ajuga pyramidalis* CARPET BUGLEWEED *A. reptans*	Low, creeping perennials that spread rapidly from stolons. Glossy green leaves rise 4 in. from the ground in A. reptans and 6 in. in A. pyramidalis; spikes of blue or lavender flowers rise above the foliage. Cultivars provide leaf and flower variations.	○ ● ●	Spring to early summer	Height: 6–10" Spread: 6–18"	4 to 9	Full sun to partial shade; grows best with some afternoon shade in warm climates. Soil should not be wet or excessively drained. Bugleweed can become weedy if planted with other border or bedding plants.
ALCHEMILLA LADY'S-MANTLE *Alchemilla vulgaris* (*A. mollis*)	A low border and edging perennial with particularly attractive, scalloped, gray-green foliage. Tiny yellow-green flowers are borne in loose, spraylike clusters above the leaves.		Spring to midsummer	Height: 8–18" Spread: 1–2'	4 to 8	Full sun to partial shade. Ordinary, evenly moist garden soil, neither very wet nor very dry. Lady's-mantle can become somewhat weedy with age and may need to be divided.
ALLIUM NODDING ONION, WILD ONION *Allium cernuum* RAMSONS ◄ *A. ursinum*	Perennials with small, elongated bulbs that produce shoots topped by umbels of 6-parted, ⅓-in. flowers. Grass-leaved A. cernuum has drooping light pink flowers, while those of broad-leaved A. ursinum are white.	○ ●	A. cern. Midsummer A. urs. Late spring to early summer	A. cern. Height: 6–24" Spread: 4–6" A. urs. Height: 6–18" Spread: 4–6"	4 to 8	Partial to full shade; A. cernuum will also grow well in full sun. Moist, well-drained, humus-rich soil. A. ursinum spreads by seeds and can become invasive.

			Flower Color	Time of Bloom	Growth Habit	Hardiness Zones	Growing Conditions
	ALNUS COMMON ALDER, BLACK ALDER *Alnus glutinosa*	A small deciduous tree or large shrub with gray bark that splits into long plates with age and 3- to 4-in., oval, toothed leaves. Red-brown male flowers cluster in 2- to 4-in.-long catkins; female flower clusters form rounded, woody cones.	●	*Early spring*	Height: 40–60' Spread: 20–40'	3 to 7	*Full sun to partial shade. Moist to wet, even water-logged, soil. There is no need to add nitrogen fertilizer since microorganisms on alder roots produce it.*
	ALOCASIA ELEPHANT'S-EAR PLANT, TARO *Alocasia macrorrhiza* ◄ *A. plumbea*	Tropical evergreen perennials grown for their large (up to 3 ft. long), arrow-head-shaped leaves with pronounced veins. The small flowers are clustered into a coblike structure. A. plumbea has a purply sheen on underside of leaves.	● ●	*Periodically in zones 10–11; no flowers when grown as an annual.*	Height: 5–15' Spread: 2–5'	10 to 11 (Grow as an annual in colder regions)	*Filtered sun to full shade. Moist, humus-rich soil. Alocasia grows best if sheltered from the wind in a warm and humid climate. It makes a good container plant.*
	AQUILEGIA COMMON COLUMBINE *Aquilegia canadensis* GARDEN COLUMBINE ◄ *A. × hybrida*	Perennials bearing attractive blue-green leaves with rounded leaflets. The native A. canadensis has red-and-yellow flowers; those of A. × hybrida come in many colors. Each flower has 5 tubular petals ending in knob-tipped spurs.	● ● ● ●	*A. canad. Mid- to late spring* *A. × hyb. Spring to early summer*	*A. canad.* Height: 1–3' Spread: 9–18" *A. × hyb.* Height: 2–3' Spread: 9–18"	*A. canad.* 3 to 8 *A. × hyb.* 3 to 9	*Full sun to partial shade. Well-drained, humus-rich soil. Hybrid columbines tend to be short-lived and should be divided every several years. Remove leaves showing leaf-miner tunnels or stems showing borer damage.*
	ASARUM EUROPEAN WILD GINGER *Asarum europaeum*	A perennial grown as a ground cover where winters are not severe. Glossy, evergreen, heart-shaped leaves arch over 3-part, 1/2-in., thimble-shaped maroon flowers. Rootstocks smell and taste like ginger.	●	*Spring*	Height: 6–9" Spread: 6–12"	5 to 9	*Partial to full shade. Moist, loamy soil that never completely dries out. Asarum is easy to grow and will spread with time.*
	ASPLENIUM MAIDENHAIR SPLEEN-WORT *Asplenium trichomanes*	A dainty evergreen fern that forms clumps of thin (5- to 8-in.-long and 3/4-in.-wide), dissected leaves. The purple-stemmed fronds have approximately 20 pairs of rounded, 1/4-in., toothed lobes.		*No flowers*	Height: 3–5" Spread: 6–15"	3 to 8	*Full shade. Moist, alkaline soil. Asplenium grows well on moss-covered limestone rocks in a shady rock garden. It grows best in cool climates.*

◄ *Indicates species shown*

Plants for American Shade Gardens

			Flower Color	Time of Bloom	Growth Habit	Hardiness Zones	Growing Conditions
	ASTILBE ◄ *Astilbe × arendsii* DWARF CHINESE ASTILBE *A. chinensis* 'Pumila'	Perennials bearing plumed sprays on stems and deep green, dissected leaves. The many cultivars range from purple to red to pink to white. The clump-forming dwarf Chinese astilbe has deep red-pink flowers.	○ ◔ ● ●	*A. × arendsii* Mid-spring to early summer *A. c.* 'Pumila' Late summer	*A. × arendsii* Height: 1½–3½' Spread: 1–2' *A. c.* 'Pumila' Height: 8–10" Spread: 6–8"	4 to 8	Filtered sun to partial shade, with some afternoon shade in warm climates. Moist, humus-rich soil. A damp, streamside site is ideal, but avoid waterlogged conditions. Astilbes are heavy feeders; fertilize or dress with compost in spring.
	ATHYRIUM JAPANESE PAINTED FERN *Athyrium goeringianum* 'Pictum'	A deciduous fern with gray-green, 1- to 1½-ft.-long fronds that are tinged with purple at the leaflet bases and then turn lavender and gray toward the tips.		No flowers	Height: 1–1½' Spread: 6–9"	3 to 8	Filtered sun to medium shade. Moist, well-drained, acidic, humus-rich soil. Japanese painted fern grows best where the climate is cool and damp. Propagate by spores in late summer.
	AUCUBA JAPANESE LAUREL *Aucuba japonica* GOLD-DUST PLANT ◄ *A. japonica* 'Gold-Dust'	An evergreen shrub with dense branches and thick 5- to 7-in.-long olive green leaves. Tiny maroon flowers produce ¾-in., bright red fruits. The leaves of A. japonica 'Gold-Dust' are speckled with yellow.	●	Late winter to early spring	Height: 5–15' Spread: 3–12'	7 to 10	Partial to full shade. Moist, well-drained, humus-rich soil. Japanese laurel is an ideal plant for shady patios because it grows well in large tubs. Propagate by seeds or semiripe cuttings in summer.
	BEGONIA HARDY BEGONIA *Begonia grandis*	A frost-sensitive perennial with tuberous roots, succulent red stems, and smooth, green, red-veined leaves. The fragrant, pink, 1½-in. flowers have 2 petals each if female and 4 if male. White-flowered cultivars are available.	○ ◔	Summer to frost	Height: 2–3' Spread: 1–2'	6 to 8 (Grow as an annual in colder regions)	Filtered sun to medium shade. Moist, humus-rich, well-drained soil. Provide mulch during winter in zones 6–7. Propagate by seeds or by division if tubers are large.
	BEGONIA WAX BEGONIA *Begonia* Semperflorens-Cultorum hybrids	An evergreen, bushy perennial with fleshy stems; round, succulent, cupped leaves; and mounds of white, pink, or red flowers in single or double form. Wax begonia blooms almost continually, and the flowering season is exceptionally long.	○ ◔ ●	Mid-spring to early autumn	Height: 8–18" Spread: 6–15"	10 to 11 (Grow as an annual in zone 9 and colder)	Full sun to shade, with some afternoon shade in warm climates. Well-drained, yet moist, soil. In cold climates, grow wax begonias outdoors until fall, then cut back, put in pots, and overwinter inside.

			Flower Color	Time of Bloom	Growth Habit	Hardiness Zones	Growing Conditions
	BEGONIA HYBRID TUBEROUS BEGONIA *Begonia* Tuberhybrida hybrids	Tuberous begonias with short stems bearing flowers up to 6 in. across in either single- or double-petaled forms. They resemble camellias, carnations, roses, or daffodils. Flower colors include white, pink, red, yellow, and orange.	○ ◐ ● ●	Summer to early autumn	Height: 2–2½' Spread: 2–2½'	9 to 11 (Grow as an annual in zone 8 and colder)	Filtered sun to medium shade. Moist, humus-rich, well-drained soil. These begonias will not grow well in waterlogged soil. Protect them from hot, drying winds. Plants can be grown indoors in containers.
	BROWALLIA BUSH VIOLET, SAPPHIRE FLOWER *Browallia speciosa*	A frost-sensitive perennial usually grown as an annual. The 4-in.-long, light green, lance-shaped leaves have darker veins. The 1- to 2-in., 5-petaled flowers are pale violet with white centers. Cultivars with blue or white flowers are available.	○ ◐ ●	Midsummer to frost	Height: 2–3' Spread: 1–1½'	10 to 11 (Grow as an annual in zone 9 and colder)	Full sun to partial shade. Moist soil rich in organic matter. Started by seeds indoors, bush violet can be grown as an annual in colder zones. Do not plant outside until all danger of frost has passed. It makes an ideal houseplant.
	BRUNNERA SIBERIAN BUGLOSS *Brunnera macrophylla*	A clump-forming perennial with large (8-in.), attractive, heart-shaped leaves. Sprays of small (¼-in.), sky blue, forget-me-not-like flowers rise above the leaves. This plant is a good ground cover for shady borders.	◐	Early to mid-spring	Height: 1–1½' Spread: 6–12"	3 to 9	Filtered sun to full shade, with some afternoon shade in warm climates; tolerates full sun in cool climates. Well-drained, evenly moist soil. Mulch during winter in zones 3–6.
	CALADIUM FANCY-LEAVED CALADIUM *Caladium × hortulanum*	A tender perennial with big (1- to 1½-ft.), arrowhead-shaped leaves variegated in red, salmon, pink, or white and held on long stalks. Coblike clusters of small flowers are largely hidden by the colorful foliage.	●	Intermittent blooming; no flowers when grown as an annual.	Height: 1–3' Spread: 1–2'	10 to 11 (Grow as an annual in zone 9 and colder)	Filtered sun to partial shade. Moist, but not wet, soil rich in humus. In spring, plant tubers in pots indoors or sow directly out-doors in warm climates. This caladium grows best in warm shade and also makes a fine houseplant.
	CALLICARPA BEAUTYBERRY ◄ *Callicarpa bodinieri* var. *giraldii* 'Profusion' JAPANESE BEAUTY-BERRY *C. japonica*	Deciduous shrubs with attractive clusters of violet, ⅛-in. berries in autumn, after the leaves have fallen. C. bodinieri has tiny, star-shaped lilac flowers; C. japonica has light pink flowers and narrower leaves than those of C. bodinieri.	○ ◐ ◐	Summer	'Profusion' Height: 5–10' Spread: 5–10' C. japonica Height: 3–5' Spread: 3–6'	5 to 8	Full sun to light shade. Moist, well-drained, humus-rich soil. Prune back stems to 6 in. from the ground in late winter; flowers are borne on new growth.

◄ Indicates species shown

Plants for American Shade Gardens

		Flower Color	Time of Bloom	Growth Habit	Hardiness Zones	Growing Conditions
CAMELLIA COMMON CAMELLIA, JAPANESE CAMELLIA *Camellia japonica*	An evergreen small tree or large shrub with dark green, glossy, elliptical leaves and showy, white, pink, or red, 3- to 5-in. flowers that can be single or double. Many cultivars are available.	○ ◐ ●	Winter	Height: 10–15' Spread: 6–10'	7 to 10	Filtered sun to partial shade. Moist, acid, humus-rich, well-drained soil. Protect from drying winds during the winter. Camellia is a shallow-rooted shrub that benefits from mulching. Scale insects and mealybugs may be problems.
CARAGANA SIBERIAN PEA TREE *Caragana arborescens*	A narrow, erect tree or large shrub that bears showy clusters of bright yellow, ³⁄4-in., pealike flowers just as its leaves emerge in the late spring. Mature leaves are 2–3½ in. long and made up of 4 to 6 pairs of leaflets. The fruit is a 2 in. long pod.		Late spring	Height: 15–20' Spread: 12–18'	2 to 7	Full sun. Well-drained, sandy soil. Caragana is quite drought tolerant once established. Its resistance to wind, salt, and poor soil makes this tree useful as a shade provider in difficult sites.
CHILOPSIS DESERT WILLOW *Chilopsis linearis*	A small deciduous tree native to the Southwest. The trunk and twisted branches have gray, shaggy bark. The 2- to 5-in.-long willowlike leaves are shed during drought. Pink, pouched, bell-shaped, 3-in. flowers produce long pods.	◐	Spring to autumn	Height: 15–25' Spread: 10–15'	7 to 11	Full sun to partial shade. Well-drained, sandy soil. A fast-growing tree when young, desert willow slows in maturity. It provides shade in hot, dry locations.
CHRYSO-GONUM GREEN-AND-GOLD, GOLDEN STAR *Chrysogonum virginianum*	A long-blooming perennial that is an excellent ground cover or bedding plant. Single, bright gold, composite flowers with pointed petals are borne on short stems above a spreading, dense mat of lustrous green leaves.		Early spring to midsummer	Height: 6–12" Spread: 6–12"	4 to 9	Full sun to medium shade, with some afternoon shade in warm climates. Well-drained, moist soil. Mulch lightly during winter in cooler climates. Remove mulch early in the spring or plants may rot. Chrysogonum is not invasive.
CIMICIFUGA BLACK SNAKEROOT *Cimicifuga racemosa* BUGBANE ◂ *C. simplex* 'White Pearl'	Woodland perennials with arching spikes of ½-in., creamy white, ill-scented flowers on long stems. The large, compound leaves are deeply lobed. Smaller than the native C. racemosa, C. simplex 'White Pearl' has pearl-like flower buds.	○	C. racem. Midsummer C. simplex Early autumn	C. racem. Height: 3–8' Spread: 1–1½' C. simplex Height: 2–4' Spread: 1–1½'	3 to 8	Full sun to partial shade, with some afternoon shade in warm climates. Moist, well-drained soil rich in organic matter. Plants grow slowly.

			Flower Color	Time of Bloom	Growth Habit	Hardiness Zones	Growing Conditions
	CLETHRA SWEET PEPPERBUSH, SUMMER-SWEET ◄ *Clethra alnifolia* *C. alnifolia* 'Hummingbird'	Deciduous shrubs with cylindrical clusters of fragrant white flowers at the branch tips. The leathery, dark green leaves turn yellow or orange in fall. *C. alnifolia is native to eastern wetlands; C. a. 'Hummingbird' is a dwarf cultivar.*	○	Mid- to late summer	*C. alnifolia* Height: 3–10' Spread: 4–6' 'Hummingbird' Height: 1–2' Spread: 4–6'	4 to 9	*Full sun to full shade. Wet, acidic, humus-rich soil.* Clethra *does not grow well where soils are seasonally dry. These are good plants for seaside plantings in wet sites.*
	COLEUS *Coleus × hybridus*	Annual or perennial plants grown more for their highly decorative, heart-shaped leaves than for the spikes of small, light blue, 2-lipped flowers. The 4-in.-long scalloped leaves come in combinations of red, green, purple, and white.	●	Late spring to late summer	Height: 1–3' Spread: 8–12"	10 to 11 (Grow as an annual in colder regions)	*Partial to full shade (in full sun the leaf colors tend to fade). Moist soil rich in humus.* Coleus *will grow as a perennial in zones 10–11. Grow from cuttings or start seeds indoors 8–10 weeks before the last frost. It is an excellent container plant.*
	CONVALLARIA LILY-OF-THE-VALLEY *Convallaria majalis*	A hardy perennial that forms a dense ground cover. It bears attractive, spear-shaped, deep green leaves and fragrant, nodding, $\frac{1}{4}$- to $\frac{1}{3}$-in., bell-shaped white flowers.	○	Late spring	Height: 6–12" Spread: 4–8"	3 to 8	*Partial to full shade. Moist, well-drained soil rich in organic matter. With age, lily-of-the-valley forms mats that should be divided and replanted to maintain vigorous growth and flowering.*
	CORNUS BUNCHBERRY *Cornus canadensis*	A flowering dogwood relative that sprawls along the ground. The 1- to 3-in.-long leaves are attached in whorls to semiwoody stems. Small, greenish white flowers, each surrounded by 4 white bracts, produce bright red, $\frac{1}{4}$-in.-wide berries.	○	Late spring	Height: 4–9" Spread: 6–24"	2 to 6	*Filtered sun to moderate shade. Moist, acidic, peaty soil. In full sun the leaves are small and stunted. Bunchberry doesn't grow well in areas where summers are hot or dry.*
	CORNUS KOUSA DOGWOOD ◄ *Cornus kousa* FLOWERING DOGWOOD *C. × rutgersensis*	Small deciduous trees grown for their flower clusters surrounded by showy white bracts, graceful branches, and attractive leaves that turn red or purple in fall. *C. kousa flowers later than C. × rutgersensis. Grow as specimen plants or massed.*	○	*C. kousa* Late spring *C. × rutger.* Mid-spring	Height: 20–30' Spread: 20–30'	5 to 9	*Full sun to partial shade. Moist, well-drained, humus-rich soil. These species do not grow well where soil is seasonally dry and hot. Trees are resistant to anthracnose fungus, which has blighted other dogwood species.*

◄ *Indicates species shown*

Plants for American Shade Gardens

		Flower Color	Time of Bloom	Growth Habit	Hardiness Zones	Growing Conditions
CORNUS CORNELIAN CHERRY DOGWOOD *Cornus mas*	A deciduous small tree or large shrub with 2- to 4-in.-long, dark green, pointed leaves and ³/₄-in. clusters of yellow flowers, each surrounded by 4 bracts that appear before the foliage in early spring. Cherry red, ¹/₂-in. fruits ripen in summer.		Early spring	Height: 20–25' Spread: 15–20'	5 to 8	Full sun to partial shade. Evenly moist, well-drained, humus-rich soil. Cornelian cherry dogwood will adapt to a wide variety of soil conditions. Remove lower branches to grow plants or grass beneath the tree's spread.
CORYDALIS PINK CORYDALIS, FUMEWORT *Corydalis bulbosa* (*C. solida*)	A perennial whose small bulbous tubers each produce a single stem bearing several feathery, gray-green leaves and a spike of 10 to 20 pink, tubular, 2-lipped, ¹/₃-in.-long flowers. Fumewort dies back to tubers in summer.	●	Early spring	Height: 4–8" Spread: 3–6"	6 to 8	Full sun to partial shade. Moist, well-drained, humus-rich soil. Fumewort will not survive long where the soil is dry.
CORYDALIS YELLOW CORYDALIS *Corydalis lutea*	An evergreen, clump-forming perennial with clusters of bright yellow, ³/₄-in., ornate flowers borne on smooth stems above soft, gray-green, fernlike foliage. Corydalis is a perfect plant for shady rock gardens or moist walls.		Mid-spring to midsummer	Height: 8–15" Spread: 6–12"	5 to 7 (Grow as an annual in zones 3 and 4)	Full sun to light shade, with some afternoon shade in warm climates. Moist, well-drained soil that is rich in organic matter. Corydalis will self-sow.
CRATAEGUS LAVALLE HAWTHORN *Crataegus × lavallei* WASHINGTON HAWTHORN ◄ *C. phaenopyrum*	Deciduous trees with bright red fruits and 2- to 4-in. thorns on their twigs. C. × lavallei has 2-in.-long, oval, toothed leaves and fruits speckled with brown. The sharp-lobed leaves of C. phaenopyrum have light undersides.	○	Mid-spring	C. × lav. Height: 15–30' Spread: 15–20' C. phaen. Height: 20–30' Spread: 15–25'	C. × lav. 5 to 7 C. phaen. 3 to 8	Full sun to light shade. Well-drained ordinary garden soil. Prune deadwood in winter, but be careful of the stiff, sharp thorns. The trees are susceptible to cedar apple rust, so do not plant near junipers.
CYCLAMEN PERSIAN VIOLET *Cyclamen cilicium* BABY CYCLAMEN ◄ *C. hederifolium*	Perennials with nodding rosy pink or white flowers whose petals sweep back from a darker-stained mouth. C. cilicium has fragrant, ³/₄-in. flowers and heart-shaped leaves. C. hederifolium has 1-in. flowers and marbled, ivy-shaped leaves.	○ ●	C. cil. Autumn C. hed. Late summer to early autumn	C. cil. Height: 3–5" Spread: 2–4" C. hed. Height: 3–4" Spread: 4–6"	5 to 9	Filtered sun to partial shade. Well-drained, evenly moist, humus-rich soil. Cyclamen tubers will often rot if the soil is wet and soggy.

		Flower Color	Time of Bloom	Growth Habit	Hardiness Zones	Growing Conditions
	CYMBALARIA KENILWORTH IVY, PENNYWORT *Cymbalaria muralis*	A creeping perennial vine with rounded, ³/₄-in., ivylike, pale green leaves and ¹/₂-in., spurred flowers that look like miniature lavender snapdragons with yellow throats. Trailing stems form new roots at bases of leaves.	●	Summer	Height: 1–2" Spread: 1–2'	7 to 10 (Grow as an annual in colder regions)	Partial to full shade. Moist, humus-rich soil. Cymbalaria will grow on shady garden walls and makes an excellent plant for shallow containers and hanging baskets. Plants can be invasive.
	CYRTOMIUM JAPANESE HOLLY FERN *Cyrtomium falcatum*	An evergreen fern with glossy, deep green, stiff, 2¹/₂-ft. fronds that resemble holly leaves. Plants are killed by light frosts, but remain evergreen when grown in warm climates or indoors.		No flowers	Height: 1–3' Spread: 1–1¹/₂'	7 to 10	Filtered sun to light shade. Humus-rich, moist, well-drained soil. Remove old fronds as they die back. Japanese holly fern can be grown as an indoor container plant during winter.
	DENNSTAED-TIA HAY-SCENTED FERN *Dennstaedtia punctilobula*	A deciduous, creeping fern native to the eastern U.S. Soft, fuzzy, 1- to 2-ft. fronds smell like freshly mowed hay if crushed. The fronds are divided into about 20 pairs of leaflets, each further subdivided, giving a lacy appearance.		No flowers	Height: 9–16" Spread: 6–9"	3 to 8	Full sun to light shade. Humus-rich soil. Hay-scented fern grows well in woodland gaps and on rocky sites. Plants spread rapidly from rootstocks and are difficult to eradicate once established.
	DICENTRA DUTCHMAN'S-BREECHES *Dicentra cucullaria*	A perennial eastern wildflower that appears before trees leaf out in spring and dies back to pink underground tubers by summer. Fleshy stalks rise above fernlike leaves bearing spurred, white, fragrant, ¹/₂- to ³/₄-in. flowers.	○	Early to mid-spring	Height: 6–12" Spread: 6–12"	3 to 7	Partial to full shade. Moist, well-drained, slightly acidic soil. Dutchman's-breeches occurs naturally in rich woodland soil.
	DICENTRA WILD BLEEDING-HEART *Dicentra eximia* WESTERN BLEEDING-HEART ◄ *D. formosa*	Native perennials with rose pink, ¹/₂-in. flowers that look like elongated hearts. The flowers are borne on erect stems that rise above mounds of fernlike, deeply cut leaves. D. formosa is preferred for the West Coast and D. eximia for the East.	●	Late spring to autumn	Height: 1–1¹/₂' Spread: 6–12"	3 to 9	Full sun to full shade, with some afternoon shade in warm climates. Moist, well-drained soil. Mulch in winter in cooler climates. Dicentra may need to be divided if it spreads too rapidly. Both species have long flowering seasons.

◄ *Indicates species shown*

Plants for American Shade Gardens

		Flower Color	Time of Bloom	Growth Habit	Hardiness Zones	Growing Conditions
DICENTRA COMMON BLEEDING-HEART *Dicentra spectabilis*	A classic border perennial with foot-long sprays of pendent, pink-and-white, 1-in., heart-shaped flowers. Lush, gray-green, dissected leaves die back in midsummer. A cultivar with pure white flowers, 'Alba', is available.	○ ●	Late spring to midsummer	Height: 1½–3' Spread: 1½–2½'	3 to 9	Partial sun to partial shade; full sun if soil is moist and climate is cool. Well-drained, evenly moist soil that is rich in humus. Avoid hot, dry sites. D. spectabilis tends to be short-lived in zones 8 and warmer.
DIGITALIS YELLOW FOXGLOVE ◄ *Digitalis grandiflora* COMMON FOXGLOVE *D. purpurea*	Biennials with rosettes of thick, soft leaves that appear the first year. Tall flower stalks appear the second year. D. grandiflora has yellow flowers with brown dots, D. purpurea has pink or white tubular flowers with contrasting dots.	○ ● ●	Late spring to midsummer	D. grand. Height: 2–3' Spread: 10–12" D. purp. Height: 2–5' Spread: 10–12"	4 to 8	Full sun to partial shade. Moist, well-drained soil. Few pests harm the leaves, the source of the drug digitalis. Foxglove self-seeds, but not always where you desire; transplant seedlings in the fall or early spring.
DRYOPTERIS MALE FERN ◄ *Dryopteris filix-mas* MARGINAL SHIELD FERN *D. marginalis*	Leathery ferns with prominent rootstocks and about 20 leaflets, each made up of about 20 subleaflets. D. filix-mas has yellow-green, semievergreen fronds, while the evergreen fronds of D. marginalis are blue-green above and light green below.		No flowers	Height: 1–2' Spread: 6–18"	3 to 8	Filtered sun to full shade. Moist, well-drained, humus-rich soil.
ENDYMION SPANISH BLUEBELL, WOOD HYACINTH *Endymion hispanicus* (Scilla campanulata)	A spring-flowering, clump-forming perennial with straplike, glossy, 1½-ft. leaves and shoots bearing many nodding, bell-shaped, ¾-in., 6-petaled, light blue flowers. Cultivars with lavender, white, or pink flowers are available.	○ ● ● ●	Late spring	Height: 1–1½' Spread: 4–6"	4 to 9	Light shade. Humus-rich, evenly moist, well-drained soil. Sandy loam is ideal.
ENKIANTHUS RED-VEIN ENKIANTHUS ◄ *Enkianthus campanulatus* ENKIANTHUS *E. cernuus*	Deciduous shrubs with bristly-edged, dark green leaves that turn brilliant yellow-orange in autumn and clusters of tiny bell-shaped flowers. E. campanulatus has yellow, red-veined flowers; those of E. cernuus are white.	○	Mid- to late spring	E. camp. Height: 8–15' Spread: 6–8' E. cern. Height: 8–10' Spread: 6–8'	4 to 7	Full sun to full shade. Moist, deep, well-drained, humus-rich soil. Adequate moisture and acid soil are essential for Enkianthus.

			Flower Color	Time of Bloom	Growth Habit	Hardiness Zones	Growing Conditions
	EPIMEDIUM BISHOP'S HAT ◄ *Epimedium grandiflorum* E. × versicolor var. 'Sulphureum'	Durable perennial ground covers with cup-shaped, long-spurred, 1- to 2-in. flowers of white, red, or violet in E. grandiflorum and yellow in E. × versicolor. The lush groups of 6 to 9 heart-shaped leaflets remain green for most of the year.	○ ● ●	Late spring	Height: 8–12" Spread: 6–12"	5 to 9	Partial to full shade. Well-drained, humus-rich soil. Once established, bishop's hat will tolerate dry conditions. Cut off old foliage in late winter before new leaves sprout.
	ERYTHRONIUM TROUT LILY, FAWN LILY *Erythronium americanum* ◄ E. 'Pagoda'	Perennials with fleshy, 3- to 6-in., lance-shaped, mottled leaves that emerge in early spring. The bright golden, 6-part flowers are borne on leafless shoots above the foliage. E. americanum has single flowers; E. 'Pagoda' has 4–10 flowers per stem.		Early to mid-spring	E. amer. Height: 3–10" Spread: 2–6" 'Pagoda' Height: 3–14" Spread: 3–8"	E. amer. 3 to 9 'Pagoda' 4 to 9	Full sun to full shade. Moist, well-drained, humus-rich soil. Trout lily thrives under deciduous trees and shrubs. Leaves quickly die back to underground corms after the flowers produce green triangular fruits.
	EUONYMUS WINTERCREEPER *Euonymus fortunei*	A woody evergreen available in vine and small shrub forms. The oblong 3/4- to 1-in. leaves are typically dark green variegated with yellow or white. The small white flowers are inconspicuous. Vine types are used as ground covers or climbers.	○	Early summer	Vine Height: 4–8' Spread: 10–20' Shrub Height: 3–6' Spread: 4–6'	5 to 9	Full sun to full shade. Well-drained, moist soil. Sow seeds outdoors in autumn. Wintercreeper is susceptible to attack by euonymus scale insects.
	FATSIA JAPANESE ARALIA *Fatsia japonica*	A small, bushy, evergreen tree grown for its dark green, leathery, palmately lobed foliage. The 16-in. leaves are deeply cut into 5 to 11 lance-shaped lobes. The umbels of small white flowers are arranged in 1½-ft.-long panicles.	○	Autumn to early winter	Height: 5–20' Spread: 3–10'	9 to 11	Partial to full shade. Moist, humus-rich, well-drained soil. Avoid wet, soggy soil. Fatsia grows best in cool weather and makes a good container plant. Prune back to encourage vigorous growth.
	FICUS CLIMBING FIG *Ficus pumila*	An evergreen vine that attaches to surfaces by roots as it climbs. Young leaves are heart-shaped but become 2- to 4-in. ovals in maturity. This fig bears pear-shaped fruits that are 2 in. long.	●	Inconspicuous flowers	Height: 1–2' Spread: 10–20'	9 to 11	Partial sun to full shade. Moist, humus-rich, well-drained soil. Climbing fig grows best on north- and east-facing surfaces out of direct sun. Cut back to the ground if necessary to discourage rampant growth.

◄ *Indicates species shown*

Plants for American Shade Gardens

	Flower Color	Time of Bloom	Growth Habit	Hardiness Zones	Growing Conditions
FOTHERGILLA DWARF FOTHERGILLA, WITCH ALDER *Fothergilla gardenii* A deciduous shrub native to the Southeast that bears frothy, brushlike, 1- to 2-in.-long clusters of white flowers before its lopsided, oval, 1- to 2-in. leaves appear in spring. The blue-green leaves turn yellow to red in autumn.	○	Early to mid-spring	Height: 2–3' Spread: 2–3'	5 to 8	Full sun to partial shade. Well-drained, acidic, peaty soil. Sandy loam is ideal.
FRAGARIA WILD STRAWBERRY, WOOD STRAWBERRY *Fragaria vesca* An ever-bearing strawberry species with ½- to ¾-in. sweet fruits from summer to frost. The leaves are dark green above and silvery below, with toothed edges, and are arranged in threes. The flowers each have 5 white, round-tipped petals.	○	Mid-spring, then periodically to early autumn	Height: 6–12" Spread: 1–2'	3 to 9	Full sun to partial shade. Acidic, well-drained, evenly moist, humus-rich soil.
FUCHSIA HARDY FUCHSIA *Fuchsia magellanica* A shrubby semiwoody perennial with slender twigs and bright green, lance-shaped leaves in pairs or threes. The single, 1-in., dangling flowers have deep red sepals and purple-blue petals.	● ●	Summer to autumn	Height: 8–12' Spread: 4–8'	7 to 10	Filtered sun to partial shade. Humus-rich, well-drained, evenly moist soil; sandy loam is ideal. Cut back in spring to encourage vigorous growth. Fuchsia grows best in cool weather and can be grown indoors in large containers.
GALANTHUS SNOWDROP *Galanthus nivalis* An early spring bulb that often flowers before the last snowfall. Shoots bear a single flower with 3 white outer segments and 3 inner segments that are white with green markings. Pairs of gray-green leaves disappear by summer.	○	Late winter to early spring	Height: 4–8" Spread: 2–3"	3 to 9	Full sun to full shade. Well-drained, evenly moist, humus-rich soil. Plant bulbs 3–4 in. deep in autumn. Snowdrops are ideal for naturalizing in woodlands; they grow well under deciduous trees and shrubs.
GALIUM SWEET WOODRUFF *Galium odoratum* An easy-to-grow perennial ground cover with 1- to 2-in. leaves arranged in whorls of 6 to 8 around the square stems. The cross-shaped, ⅓-in. white flowers are borne in loose clusters above the foliage. All parts of the plant are fragrant.	○	Spring	Height: 8–12" Spread: 6–12"	4 to 8	Partial shade. Well-drained, evenly moist soil. Sweet woodruff may spread rapidly and become weedy in sites with abundant organic matter and moisture.

		Flower Color	Time of Bloom	Growth Habit	Hardiness Zones	Growing Conditions
	GAULTHERIA WINTERGREEN, TEABERRY *Gaultheria procumbens*	○	Early to midsummer	Height: 2–4" Spread: 4–8"	3 to 8	Filtered to full shade, but grows best in sunny patches. Dry or wet, acid, humus-rich soil. Wintergreen makes a good ground cover.
	GENTIANA CLOSED GENTIAN *Gentiana andrewsii* CRESTED GENTIAN ◄ *G. septemfida*	●	Late summer to early autumn	G. andr. Height: 1–3' Spread: 1–2' G. sept. Height: 10–15" Spread: 6–12"	G. andr. 3 to 9 G. sept. 6 to 8	Full sun to partial shade. Moist soil. G. andrewsii thrives in soggy soil; G. septemfida grows best in well-drained, humus-rich soil. Propagate by division in spring, or sow seeds in fall; divide and replant every 3 years in fresh soil.
	GERANIUM HARDY GERANIUM ◄ *Geranium himalayense* 'Johnson's Blue' BIG-ROOT CRANESBILL *G. macrorrhizum*	●●●	Late summer to autumn	Height: 8–18" Spread: 1–1½'	3 to 9	Full sun to partial shade, with some afternoon shade in warm climates. Well-drained soil that is moist and rich in organic matter.
	GERANIUM BLOOD-RED GERANIUM, LANCASTER GERANIUM *Geranium sanguineum* var. *striatum*	●	Summer	Height: 4–8" Spread: 1–1½'	4 to 8	Full sun to partial shade, with some afternoon shade in warm climates. Well-drained soil that is moist and rich in organic matter. This geranium spreads slowly with time.
	GLEDITSIA THORNLESS HONEY LOCUST ◄ *Gleditsia triacanthos* var. *inermis* *G. triacanthos* var. *inermis* 'Shademaster'		Mid- to late spring	Height: 30–70' Spread: 20–30'	3 to 9	Full sun. Moist, well-drained, humus-rich, alkaline soil. Honey locust is drought tolerant once established and adaptable to a wide variety of conditions. Trees provide filtered shade. The locust borer may be a problem.

GAULTHERIA — A low, evergreen plant with ½-in., urn-shaped, pendent white flowers producing ¼-in. red berries that last into winter. Wintergreen-flavored leaves are bright green when young but become leathery and turn reddish in autumn.

GENTIANA — Perennials with deep blue flowers borne in whorled clusters near the tips of branched stems. Flowers of the native G. andrewsii appear to be always in bud, while the evergreen G. septemfida has open, pointed, 5-petaled flowers.

GERANIUM — Hardy perennials with showy, 5-petaled flowers borne on long stalks above mounds of 5-lobed, dissected, deep green leaves. 'Johnson's Blue' has violet flowers with purple veins; G. macrorrhizum has magenta flowers.

GERANIUM — A hardy, hummock-forming perennial with 5-lobed, deeply dissected, dark green leaves. The showy, cup-shaped, 5-petaled flowers are pink with darker veins. The plant is often sold as G. s. 'Lancastriense.'

GLEDITSIA — Large trees whose 6- to 8-in., doubly compound leaves each have about 100 leaflets. Pendent clusters of small yellow-green flowers produce 8- to 18-in., flattened brown pods. 'Shademaster' is a fast-growing cultivar that lacks pods.

◄ *Indicates species shown*

Plants for American Shade Gardens

			Flower Color	Time of Bloom	Growth Habit	Hardiness Zones	Growing Conditions
	GUNNERA *Gunnera manicata*	A clump-forming perennial with dramatic, rhubarblike, 3- to 8-ft. leaves. Conical, foot-long spikes of light green, petalless flowers produce clusters of orange-red fruits.	●	Early summer	Height: 5–10' Spread: 6–7'	8 to 11	Full sun to light shade. Moist, humus-rich soil. Gunnera is ideal for pond, pool, or streamside planting. Provide winter mulch in zone 8.
	HALESIA CAROLINA SILVER-BELL *Halesia carolina*	A small deciduous tree native to the Carolinas with dark green, 2- to 4-in. leaves that turn yellow in autumn. It bears clusters of white, drooping, ½- to ¾-in., bell-shaped flowers.	○	Mid-spring	Height: 30–40' Spread: 20–35'	4 to 8	Full sun to partial shade in acidic, deep, well-drained, evenly moist, humus-rich soil. Carolina silver-bell makes a beautiful shade tree or addition to a woodland border. When grown in its preferred conditions, it is a low-maintenance species.
	HAMAMELIS WITCH HAZEL *Hamamelis × intermedia* ◀ *H. virginiana*	Vigorous flowering shrubs with distinctive straplike petals. Cultivars have flower colors from yellow to red, and fall leaf colors from yellow to burgundy. H. virginiana has fragrant blooms; witch hazel extract is made from its stems and roots.	●	H. × inter. Late winter to early spring H. virg. Autumn	H. × inter. Height: 15–20' Spread: 6–12' H. virg. Height: 20–30' Spread: 10–20'	H. × inter. 5 to 9 H. virg. 3 to 8	Full sun to partial shade. Moist, well-drained, slightly acidic soil rich in organic matter. No serious diseases or insect pests bother witch hazel.
	HEDERA ENGLISH IVY *Hedera helix*	An evergreen perennial vine with dark green, leathery, roughly triangular leaves. The many cultivars vary in leaf lobes, variegation, and hardiness; those with darker leaves do best in the shade. Grow ivy as a ground cover, vine, or houseplant.	●	Mid-autumn	Height: 3"–30' Spread: 1–15'	4 to 9	Full sun to shade, with some afternoon shade in warm climates. Moist, well-drained, humus-rich soil. English ivy is not particular about soil acidity. Select hardy cultivars such as 'Bulgaria' for cold regions.
	HELLEBORUS CHRISTMAS ROSE *Helleborus niger* LENTEN ROSE ◀ *H. orientalis*	Evergreen perennials with deeply divided, glossy leaves and single, waxy, 1- to 1½-in., cup-shaped flowers on sturdy stems. H. niger has white fall flowers, sometimes tinged with pink; H. orientalis has white, pink, or purple spring flowers.	○ ● ●	Late autumn to late spring	Height: 1–2' Spread: 6–12"	4 to 8	Full sun in winter; partial shade in summer. Well-drained, evenly moist soil enriched with humus and limestone. Mulch Helleborus in winter in zones 4–5. Mildew and slugs can be problems.

			Flower Color	Time of Bloom	Growth Habit	Hardiness Zones	Growing Conditions
	HEPATICA LIVERLEAF, SHARP-LOBED HEPATICA *Hepatica acutiloba*	A perennial with leathery, evergreen, 3-lobed, 2-in.-long leaves that are wider than they are long. White, light blue, or pink flowers have 5–18 petals and are borne on hairy stems. The flowers open in sun and close on cloudy days.	○ ● ●	Early spring to early summer	Height: 3–4" Spread: 3–6"	3 to 7	Light shade to full shade. Neutral to alkaline, moist soil that is rich in humus. Hepatica grows well under deciduous trees and shrubs, whose fallen leaves provide a natural mulch.
	HEUCHERA ALUMROOT, ROCK GERANIUM ◀ *Heuchera americana* *H. villosa*	Evergreen perennials grown more for the mounds of foliage than for the small, greenish white flowers. The rounded leaves of H. americana emerge mottled, turn uniform green, then redden in winter. H. villosa has more triangular, green leaves.	○	H. americana Late spring to early summer H. villosa Midsummer to early autumn	Height: 2–3' Spread: 1–2'	H. amer. 4 to 6 H. vill. 5 to 7	Light shade. Well-drained, sandy, humus-rich soil; tolerates dry conditions once established. Heucheras make ideal ground covers for woodlands. Divide plants every 3–4 years.
	HOSTA PLANTAIN LILY *Hosta fortunei*	Perennials that are favorites for shade gardens. The oval or heart-shaped foliage comes in various shades of green. The 2-in. spikes of lavender flowers rise above the clumps of leaves. Cultivars vary in shape, size, and leaf variegation.	●	Late spring to early summer	Height: 1–3' Spread: 1–2'	3 to 9	Partial to full shade; full sun if soil is sufficiently moist. Evenly moist, humus-rich, well-drained soil. Hostas are prone to rotting if the soil is not well drained. Mulch during winter in cooler climates. Slugs and deer may eat leaves.
	HOSTA HOSTA HYBRIDS *Hosta* 'Krossa Regal' ◀ *H.* 'Sum and Substance'	Large hostas with bold clumps of foliage and tall spikes of lavender flowers. 'Krossa Regal' has light blue-green, pointed leaves; 'Sum and Substance' has 2-ft.-wide, yellow-green leaves that become golden yellow if grown in more sun.	●	H. 'Krossa' Midsummer to early autumn H. 'Sum' Late summer	Height: 2–3' Spread: 1½–2½'	3 to 9	Partial to full shade; full sun if soil is sufficiently moist. Evenly moist, humus-rich, well-drained soil. Hostas are prone to rotting if the soil is not well drained. Mulch during winter in cooler climates. Slugs and deer may eat leaves.
	HOSTA FRAGRANT PLANTAIN LILY *Hosta plantaginea*	A hosta bearing spikes of fragrant, 4- to 5-in., white, trumpet-shaped flowers. The 10-in.-long, glossy, light green leaves form domed mats.	○	Late summer to autumn	Height: 1½–2½' Spread: 1½–2½'	3 to 9	Partial to full shade; full sun if soil is sufficiently moist. Evenly moist, humus-rich, well-drained soil. Hostas are prone to rotting if the soil is not well drained. Mulch during winter in cooler climates. Slugs and deer may eat leaves.

◀ *Indicates species shown*

Plants for American Shade Gardens

		Flower Color	Time of Bloom	Growth Habit	Hardiness Zones	Growing Conditions
HOSTA *Hosta sieboldiana*	A hosta with attractive, gray-green, deeply ribbed, thick foliage and short spikes of pale lilac, 1½-in. flowers. Cultivars with variegated leaves are available.	●	Spring to early summer	Height: 1½–2½' Spread: 1½–2½'	3 to 9	Partial to full shade; full sun if soil is sufficiently moist. Evenly moist, humus-rich, well-drained soil. Hostas are prone to rotting if the soil is not well drained. Mulch during winter in cooler climates. Slugs and deer may eat leaves.
HYDRANGEA HORTENSIA, LACE-CAP HYDRANGEA ◄ *Hydrangea macrophylla* OAKLEAF HYDRANGEA *H. quercifolia*	Deciduous shrubs grown for their showy flower clusters and large, 6- to 8-in. leaves. H. macrophylla is evergreen where winters are mild and has pink, white, or blue flowers depending on soil pH; H. quercifolia has white flowers.	○ ● ●	Mid- to late summer	H. macro. Height: 3–6' Spread: 3–6' H. quer. Height: 4–6' Spread: 3–5'	5 to 9	Full sun to light shade. Moist, well-drained soil. Prune in autumn after flowering. Hydrangeas are often killed to the ground by severe winters.
HYPOESTES POLKA-DOT PLANT *Hypoestes phyllostachya*	A tender perennial grown for its pointed, oval, 2- to 3-in. evergreen leaves that are polka-dotted with splotches of pink. Lavender flowers appear in the leaf axils, but do not emerge when the plant is grown as an annual.	●	Summer	Height: 1–3' Spread: 1–2'	9 to 11 (Grow as an annual in colder regions)	Full sun to light shade. Well-drained, moist, humus-rich soil with additional fertilizer added periodically. Propagate Hypoestes by cuttings, or start seeds indoors 8–10 weeks before the last frost. Pinch stem tips to make the plant bushy.
ILEX MESERVE HOLLY ◄ *Ilex × meserveae* AMERICAN HOLLY *I. opaca*	Evergreen shrubs or small trees with dark green, spiny leaves and red fruits on male plants. I. × meserveae is shrubby with lustrous, 1- to 2-in., oval leaves. I. opaca is a conical tree with 2- to 4-in., dull green leaves. Many cultivars are available.	○	Mid-spring	I. × meser. Height: 7–12' Spread: 5–15' I. opaca Height: 40–50' Spread: 20–40'	I. × meser. 5 to 7 I. opaca 5 to 9	Full sun to full shade. Evenly moist, well-drained, acidic, humus-rich soil. Plant at least 1 male for every few female plants. Both holly species are resistant to salt spray.
IMPATIENS *Impatiens wallerana*	A tender perennial grown for its showy, 1- to 2-in., soft-petaled flowers in white, pink, rose, peach, yellow, orange, lilac, magenta, and dark red. Single- or double-flowered and bicolored forms are available.	○ ● ● ●	Late spring to frost	Height: 6–18" Spread: 6–12"	10 to 11 (Grow as an annual in colder regions)	Full sun to partial shade. Fertile, well-drained soil with ample moisture. Start indoors in cold regions, and set young plants outside after danger of frost has passed. Impatiens makes an excellent bedding plant.

			Flower Color	Time of Bloom	Growth Habit	Hardiness Zones	Growing Conditions
	ITEA SWEETSPIRE, VIRGINIA WILLOW *Itea virginica* ◄ *I. virginica* 'Henry's Garnet'	A perennial shrub native to the Southeast. Bright green, 4-in., oblong leaves turn bright red to burgundy in autumn. The fragrant white flowers are held in upright, hairy, 4- to 6-in. clusters.	○	*Mid-spring to early summer*	Height: 3–10' Spread: 2–6'	5 to 9	*Full sun to shade. Humus-rich, moist to wet soil.*
	KALMIA MOUNTAIN LAUREL *Kalmia latifolia*	A handsome evergreen shrub native to the East. Leathery, lustrous, 2- to 4-in., strap-like leaves are obscured in late spring by showy clusters of 1-in., purple-spotted, cuplike, white, pink, or rose flowers. It naturalizes well in woodland settings.	○ ◐ ●	*Late spring to early summer*	Height: 4–15' Spread: 2–10'	4 to 9	*Full sun to full shade; plants need shade where summers are hot. Acidic, cool, well-drained but evenly moist soil. Mountain laurel will not grow if the soil is alkaline. Protect plants from drying winter winds.*
	KOELREU-TERIA GOLDEN-RAIN TREE, VARNISH TREE *Koelreuteria paniculata*	A deciduous tree with large (14-in.-long) leaves divided into 7 to 15 leaflets. Dense, 12- to 15-in. spikes of bright yellow, ½-in. flowers produce green fruit pods that turn brown in autumn.		*Summer*	Height: 30–40' Spread: 30–45'	5 to 9	*Full sun. Ordinary, well-drained soil. Golden-rain tree will withstand heat and drought. It makes an excellent shade tree.*
	LAMIUM SPOTTED DEAD NETTLE *Lamium maculatum*	A creeping perennial with 1- to 2-in., lustrous, attractively variegated leaves and clusters of rosy pink or lavender, 1- to 2-in., double-lipped flowers. Cultivars with white flowers and variegated leaf patterns are available.	○ ◐ ◐	*Late spring to summer*	Height: 6–12" Spread: 6–8"	4 to 9	*Dappled sun to partial shade. Well-drained, moist soil. With time the plant spreads. Spotted dead nettle makes an attractive ground cover but can be invasive.*
	LEUCOTHOE DOG-HOBBLE, FETTERBUSH *Leucothoe fontanesiana*	An evergreen shrub with lustrous, dark green, 2- to 5-in., lance-shaped leaves that turn bronze in winter. Gracefully arching branches bear racemes of drooping, fragrant, white, waxy, ¼-in. flowers. Leucothoe is native to the Southeast.	○	*Mid-spring*	Height: 3–6' Spread: 3–6'	4 to 8	*Partial to full shade. Moist, well-drained, acid soil. Dog-hobble will not tolerate drought or windy sites. Prune after flowering, removing old wood to promote growth. Leaf spot, caused by fungi, can be a problem.*

◄ *Indicates species shown*

Plants for American Shade Gardens

			Flower Color	Time of Bloom	Growth Habit	Hardiness Zones	Growing Conditions
	LILIUM CANADA LILY, MEADOW LILY ◄ *Lilium canadense* TURK'S-CAP LILY *L. superbum*	Tall perennials with large, light to dark orange flowers that are often tinged with red and dotted with purple. L. canadense *has 2- to 3-in., dangling, bell-shaped flowers. The 3- to 5-in. flowers of* L. superbum *have bent-back petals.*	●	Early summer to midsummer	L. canad. Height: 3–5' Spread: 1–3' L. superb. Height: 5–8' Spread: 1–3'	L. canad. 3 to 8 L. superb. 5 to 8	*Full sun to light shade. Moist, acidic, humus-rich, fertile soil. These lilies will grow in wet meadows and boggy habitats. Propagate by dividing the scaly bulbs in autumn; plant the scale segments about 1–2 in. deep.*
	LIRIOPE BIG BLUE LILYTURF *Liriope muscari* CREEPING LILYTURF ◄ *L. spicata*	*Evergreen perennials with blue-green, 1- to 2-ft.-long, grasslike leaves and spikes of hyacinth-like flowers that rise above the mounds of foliage in summer.* L. muscari *has purple flowers;* L. spicata *has paler violet flowers.*	○ ● ● ●	Midsummer	L. musc. Height: 8–18" Spread: 1–2' L. spic. Height: 5–10" Spread: 1–2'	5 to 10	*Full sun to light shade. Evenly moist, well-drained soil. Once established, lily-turf grows well in dry soils. Cut back old leaves in early spring.*
	LOBELIA CARDINAL FLOWER *Lobelia cardinalis*	*A perennial often grown as an annual bearing striking red, double-lipped flowers atop erect stems. The 1½- to 2-in. flowers are pollinated by hummingbirds, attracted by the red color and sweet nectar. A pink-flowered cultivar exists.*	● ●	Late summer to early autumn	Height: 1–5' Spread: 6–18"	2 to 9 (Grow as an annual in colder regions)	*Full sun to full shade. Moist to wet, humus-rich soil. Cardinal flower is not difficult to grow but prone to root damage where winters are severe. Mulch over winter in colder zones. This is a wonderful plant for shady streamsides.*
	LOBELIA EDGING LOBELIA *Lobelia erinus*	*A favorite annual for edging and borders. It forms sprawling mounds of small, linear leaves. Bright blue, double-lipped flowers with contrasting white or yellow centers nestle in the foliage. Many cultivars are available.*	○ ●	Late spring to late summer	Height: 3–8" Spread: 8–10"	Hardy annual	*Full sun to partial shade, with afternoon shade in zone 8 and warmer. Average to moist, well-drained soil. Start seeds indoors 10–12 weeks before the last frost. Edging lobelia grows best in cool weather.*
	LOBELIA GREAT BLUE LOBELIA *Lobelia siphilitica*	*A clump-forming native perennial bearing densely clustered, 1-in.-long, light blue, double-lipped flowers in spikes above rosettes of lance-shaped, 2- to 4-in., light green, toothed leaves. White-flowered cultivars are available.*	○ ●	Late summer to early autumn	Height: 1–3' Spread: 8–16"	5 to 8	*Full sun to full shade. Moist to wet, slightly acidic, humus-rich soil. Great blue lobelia is an ideal plant for wet or even boggy sites.*

			Flower Color	Time of Bloom	Growth Habit	Hardiness Zones	Growing Conditions
	LYSIMACHIA CREEPING JENNIE, MONEYWORT *Lysimachia nummularia*	A creeping perennial with trailing, rooted stems bearing pairs of penny-sized, round, smooth, pale yellow leaves that turn darker green in the shade. Single, ¹/₂-in., bright yellow, cup-shaped flowers have 5 petals.		Late spring to midsummer	Height: 1–2" Spread: 1–3'	4 to 8	Full sun to partial shade. Moist, humus-rich soil. Lysimachia *is easy to grow and adaptable to a wide variety of soils, as long as they are moist to wet. With time, plants can become invasive. In humid regions they can become weedy.*
	MAGNOLIA SAUCER MAGNOLIA ◄ *Magnolia × soulangiana* STAR MAGNOLIA *M. stellata*	Small deciduous trees with lovely white flowers. The 5- to 6-in., chalice-shaped flowers of M. × soulangiana are tinged with purple. The abundant, fragrant, 3-in. flowers of M. stellata *have narrow, daisylike petals.*	○	Early to mid-spring	M. × soul. Height: 20–30' Spread: 15–30' M. stell. Height: 15–20' Spread: 10–15'	M. × soul. 5 to 9 M. stell. 3 to 8	Full sun to partial shade. Humus-rich, acid, evenly moist, well-drained soil. These magnolias are sensitive to ice damage and late-spring frosts. Protect from dry winter winds.
	MAHONIA OREGON GRAPE *Mahonia aquifolium* LEATHERLEAF MAHONIA ◄ *M. bealei*	Evergreen shrubs bearing showy clusters of small yellow flowers and glossy compound leaves that resemble American holly. Both plants bear prominent clusters of dark blue-green berries from midsummer to fall.		M. aquif. Early to mid-spring M. beal. Midwinter to early spring	M. aquif. Height: 3–6' Spread: 3–5' M. beal. Height: 10–12' Spread: 8–10'	M. aquif. 5 to 9 M. beal. 6 to 9	Light shade to full shade. Moist, well-drained, acid, humus-rich soil. These mahonias prefer a moist woodland setting. Protect from dry winter winds and sun. Use M. bealei *in southern zones only.*
	MATTEUCCIA OSTRICH FERN *Matteuccia struthiopteris*	A fern with striking, erect outer fronds resembling ostrich plumes. Up to 5 ft. tall, these fronds form a green basket around the 2-ft., dark brown, feathery, spore-bearing fronds. Large, beautiful fiddleheads emerge in spring.		No flowers	Height: 3–5' Spread: 1¹/₂–2¹/₂'	3 to 8	Full sun to medium shade. Moist to wet, humus-rich soil. Plants spread by underground runners. Ostrich fern is ideal for swampy areas and naturalizing in wet woods.
	MELIA CHINABERRY *Melia azedarach*	A deciduous tree with a spreading crown bearing 1- to 2-ft.-long leaves with many 1-in. leaflets. Fragrant, ³/₄-in., lilac or pink flowers have 5 pointed petals each and are massed in 8- to 16-in.-long clusters. Orange, ¹/₂-in. fruits appear in fall.	● ●	Mid-spring	Height: 25–40' Spread: 15–25'	7 to 10	Full sun. Adaptable to a wide variety of soils. Chinaberry has become somewhat weedy in the Southeast.

◄ *Indicates species shown*

Plants for American Shade Gardens

		Flower Color	Time of Bloom	Growth Habit	Hardiness Zones	Growing Conditions
MERTENSIA VIRGINIA BLUEBELLS *Mertensia virginica*	A strikingly beautiful native of moist, deciduous woodlands. Sprays of delicate flowers are pink in bud and powder blue in full flower, fading to pink with age. By midsummer the entire top of the plant dies back and disappears.	●	Mid- to late spring	Height: 1–2' Spread: 1–1½'	3 to 9	Full sun to partial shade. Needs well-drained soil rich in organic matter and moist throughout the growing season; will not tolerate dry conditions. Virginia bluebells may be troubled by slugs and snails.
MICROBIOTA RUSSIAN ARBORVITAE *Microbiota decussata*	A sprawling conifer that forms a trailing ground cover with plumelike branches of scalelike, yellow-green leaves and light brown, round cones. The foliage darkens to a coppery brown in winter.		No flowers	Height: 1–2' Spread: 6–15'	2 to 8	Full sun to light shade, with midday shade in regions where summers are hot. Average garden soil. Once established Microbiota is quite drought tolerant. It grows well in a container.
MONARDA BEEBALM, BERGAMOT *Monarda didyma*	A perennial that attracts hummingbirds, bees, and butterflies with its clusters of red, tubular flowers on slender, square stems. Pairs of lance-shaped leaves with a citrusy fragrance clasp the stem. White, pink, and lavender cultivars available.	○ ● ● ●	Early to late summer	Height: 2–3' Spread: 6–12"	4 to 8	Full sun to partial shade. Moist (or even wet), well-drained, humus-rich soil. Will tolerate very wet soils. Beebalm is prone to mildew when crowded. Divide plants periodically to maintain vigor and keep in check.
MYOSOTIS FORGET-ME-NOT *Myosotis scorpioides*	An early-spring-blooming perennial with clusters of clear blue, 5-petaled flowers that have yellow or white centers. The light green leaves and stems are mat forming.	●	Early spring to midsummer	Height: 3–6" Spread: 1–2'	3 to 9	Dappled sun to partial shade, with some afternoon shade in warm climates. Well-drained, evenly moist soil. Myosotis does not tolerate drought well. Plants spread rapidly in moist, shady sites, and grow well alongside shallow water.
NANDINA HEAVENLY BAMBOO *Nandina domestica*	A member of the barberry family whose textured, evergreen foliage reddens in autumn. The pointed, 1- to 2-in. leaflets resemble bamboo leaves. The 6- to 12-in.-long flower clusters are borne at the branch tips. Shiny red berries follow.	○	Late spring to early summer	Height: 3–8' Spread: 2–4'	7 to 11	Full sun to light shade. Moist, well-drained, acid soil. Once established, plants are quite drought tolerant. Heavenly bamboo grows slowly.

		Flower Color	Time of Bloom	Growth Habit	Hardiness Zones	Growing Conditions
NARCISSUS DAFFODIL *Narcissus pseudonarcissus*	Among the most beloved of the springtime bulbs. The 2-in. yellow trumpet petal is surrounded by 6 frilled, pointed lobes. There are hundreds of daffodil cultivars and hybrids to choose from with a range of colors and spring flowering times.	○	Early to mid-spring	Height: 8–18" Spread: 6–12"	3 to 9	Full sun to semishade. Likes well-drained, fertile soil kept moist during the spring flowering season. Do not trim back leaves until they have turned brown and withered. Larger types are good for naturalizing. Divide when too dense.
NEPHROLEPIS SWORD FERN *Nephrolepis cordifolia*	A semievergreen fern with 1- to 2-ft.-long and 1- to 2-in.-wide arching fronds arising from rootstocks that have small tubers attached. The round-tipped, finely toothed leaflets are set close together and sometimes overlap.		No flowers	Height: 1–2' Spread: 6–12"	10 to 11	Partial to full shade. Well-drained, evenly moist, humus-rich soil. Sword fern can be grown as an indoor container plant in regions with cold winters. Divide rootstocks in early fall.
ONOCLEA SENSITIVE FERN *Onoclea sensibilis*	A fern whose broadly triangular, arching, 1½-ft. fronds have up to 12 pairs of wavy-edged, fingerlike leaflets that turn an attractive yellowish brown with the first frost. Spores are borne in tiny, grapelike clusters on separate, 1-ft. fronds.		No flowers	Height: 1–2' Spread: 1–2'	3 to 8	Full sun to medium shade. Moist to wet, humus-rich soil. Sensitive fern spreads by stout rootstocks and may be difficult to eradicate if it becomes invasive.
OSMUNDA CINNAMON FERN ◄ *Osmunda cinnamomea* ROYAL FERN *O. regalis*	Attractive mid-sized ferns with sterile green fronds that grow around cinnamon brown fertile fronds, which appear in spring at the center of the clump. The fronds have rounded leaflet lobes. Young fronds of O. cinnamomea are edible.		No flowers	O. cinn. Height: 1½–2½' Spread: 1–1½' O. reg. Height: 4–6' Spread: 2–3'	3 to 8	Full sun to partial shade. Moist to wet, acid soil that is rich in organic matter. Both species spread very slowly.
OXYDENDRUM SOURWOOD *Oxydendrum arboreum*	A medium-sized deciduous tree native to the East with branches that droop toward the tips and a narrowly pyramidal crown. It bears clusters of fragrant, white, bell-shaped flowers. Leaves turn yellow, red, and purple in autumn.	○	Mid- to late summer	Height: 25–60' Spread: 15–25'	6 to 9	Full sun to partial shade. Humus-rich, well-drained, moist, acid soil.

◄ Indicates species shown

Plants for American Shade Gardens

		Flower Color	Time of Bloom	Growth Habit	Hardiness Zones	Growing Conditions
PACHY-SANDRA ALLEGHANY SPURGE *Pachysandra procumbens* JAPANESE SPURGE ◄ *P. terminalis*	Slow-growing, low ground covers with whorls of dark, lustrous, evergreen leaves. Plants produce short spikes of creamy white flowers after the new leaves appear in spring. Cultivars with variegated leaves are available.	○	Early spring to early summer	Height: 6–12" Spread: 1–2'	3 to 9	Full sun to deep shade, with some afternoon shade in warm climates; in all climates, partial shade produces the best growth. Well-drained, moist, fertile soil with ample organic matter.
PELTI-PHYLLUM UMBRELLA PLANT *Peltiphyllum peltatum*	A Pacific Coast native grown for its large (10-in.), rounded leaves cut into 10 to 15 deep lobes. Domed, 2- to 6-in. clusters of ¼-in., light pink or white flowers appear before the foliage.	○ ◐	Spring	Height: 3–5' Spread: 1½–2'	5 to 9	Full sun to full shade. Moist, humus-rich soil. Umbrella plant is easy to grow as long as sufficient moisture is available. It may be invasive.
PHLOX BLUE PHLOX, WILD SWEET WILLIAM ◄ *Phlox divaricata* CREEPING PHLOX *P. stolonifera*	Creeping perennials with fragrant lavender-blue flowers and oval leaves. P. divaricata bears loose clusters of 1½-in. flowers with notched petals on upright stems; the mat-forming P. stolonifera has 1-in. flowers with smooth-edged petals.	◐	Early spring to early summer	P. divar. Height: 8–18" Spread: 8–12" P. stolon. Height: 4–6" Spread: 1–2'	4 to 8	Filtered sun to full shade. Well-drained, evenly moist, humus-rich, slightly acid soil. These phlox species are excellent plants for shady rock gardens or naturalizing in woodland settings.
PIERIS MOUNTAIN PIERIS ◄ *Pieris floribunda* LILY-OF-THE-VALLEY BUSH *P. japonica*	Evergreen shrubs with lustrous, 1- to 3-in.-long, finely toothed, dark green leaves. Spreading branches bear 3- to 6-in.-long clusters of ¼-in., white, fragrant, urn-shaped flowers.	○	Early spring	P. florib. Height: 2–6' Spread: 2–6' P. japon. Height: 9–12' Spread: 6–8'	P. florib. 4 to 8 P. japon. 5 to 8	Full sun to partial shade. Moist, acid, well-drained, humus-rich soil. Shelter from drying winter winds. Prune in late spring after flowering.
POLEMONIUM JACOB'S-LADDER, GREEK VALERIAN ◄ *Polemonium caeruleum* CREEPING POLEMONIUM *P. reptans*	Native perennials with pinnately divided, ladderlike leaves on the lower halves of long stems. Bell-shaped, blue (or sometimes white), 5-petaled, ½-in. flowers cluster loosely at stem tops. P. reptans is a smaller plant, growing to about 1 ft. tall.	○ ●	Late spring to late summer	Height: 1–2½' Spread: 8–12"	2 to 7	Full sun to partial shade. Well-drained, evenly moist soil that is rich in humus. Mulch Polemonium during winter in cooler climates.

			Flower Color	Time of Bloom	Growth Habit	Hardiness Zones	Growing Conditions
	POLYGO-NATUM SOLOMON'S-SEAL *Polygonatum biflorum* FRAGRANT SOLOMON'S-SEAL ◄ *P. odoratum*	Native perennials grown for the attractive pairs of ⅓-in., blue-black berries as much as the ¾-in., yellow-green, tubular flowers that dangle below arching stems. P. odoratum *has fragrant flowers and comes in a variegated cultivar.*		Spring	Height: 1–2½' Spread: 1–1½'	3 to 8	Partial sun to full shade. Well-drained soil rich in organic matter, kept evenly moist throughout the growing season. Plants may be troubled by slugs and snails.
	POLYPODIUM COMMON POLYPODY, WALL FERN *Polypodium vulgare*	An evergreen fern with lustrous, dark green, slender fronds. The 6- to 12-in., lance-shaped leaves are cut into 10 to 20 pairs of smooth-edged leaflets. Polypody is native to the cooler sections of the Northern Hemisphere.		No flowers	Height: 3–9" Spread: 6–18"	4 to 8	Partial to full shade. Humus-rich, constantly moist soil. Grow wall ferns over shady, moist rock surfaces and boulders.
	POLYSTICHUM CHRISTMAS FERN *Polystichum acrostichoides*	A medium-sized, handsome, evergreen fern with lustrous, dark green leaves that are 1 to 3 ft. long and 3 to 6 in. wide. The fronds are cut into 20 to 40 pairs of hollylike leaflets with fine bristles on their tips. Christmas ferns are excellent for cutting.		No flowers	Height: 1–2' Spread: 1–1½'	3 to 9	Filtered sun to full shade. Humus-rich soil. Christmas ferns are adaptable to both acid and alkaline soils as well as moisture conditions from swampy to evenly moist and well drained.
	PRIMULA JAPANESE PRIMROSE *Primula japonica* ◄ *P. sieboldii*	Perennials with showy, 5-petaled flowers that grow on slender stems above rosettes of long, spatula-shaped leaves. Primulas come in many different color forms. P. japonica *is taller but has smaller flowers than P. sieboldii.*	○ ◐ ●	P. japon. Late spring to early summer P. sieb. Mid-spring	P. japon. Height: 1–2' Spread: 6–12" P. sieb. Height: 6–12" Spread: 6–12"	P. japon. 4 to 9 P. sieb. 3 to 9	Partial sun to partial shade. Well-drained, constantly moist, humus-rich soil; primulas will not tolerate dry conditions. Mulch during winter in cooler climates. Plants may be troubled by slugs and snails.
	PRIMULA POLYANTHUS PRIMROSE *Primula × polyantha*	Hybrid primroses with a staggering array of flower colors, either single or in contrasting patterns. A 6- to 10-in. flower stem rises above rosettes of crinkle-surfaced, light green leaves and bears a cluster of 1- to 1½-in. flowers.	○ ◐ ◐ ● ●	Spring	Height: 1–2' Spread: 6–12"	4 to 9	Partial sun to partial shade. Well-drained, constantly moist, humus-rich soil; primulas will not tolerate dry conditions. Mulch during winter in cooler climates. Plants may be troubled by slugs and snails.

◄ *Indicates species shown*

Plants for American Shade Gardens

		Flower Color	Time of Bloom	Growth Habit	Hardiness Zones	Growing Conditions
PRIMULA COWSLIP *Primula veris* ENGLISH PRIMROSE *P. vulgaris*	Primroses with characteristic rosettes of 6- to 8-in.-long leaves and yellow flowers that rise above the foliage. P. veris has clusters of ½-in., fragrant, bright yellow flowers; P. vulgaris has individual, pale yellow, 1-in. flowers.		Spring	Height: 6–10" Spread: 4–8"	3 to 8	Partial sun to partial shade. Well-drained, constantly moist, humus-rich soil; primulas will not tolerate dry conditions. Mulch during winter in zone 4 and colder. Plants may be troubled by slugs and snails.
PRUNUS CHERRY LAUREL *Prunus laurocerasus*	An evergreen shrub with 2- to 6-in., smooth, lustrous, dark green leaves with small teeth on their edges. Fragrant, ¼-in., white flowers in 2- to 5-in.-long clusters produce dark purple, ⅓- to ½-in. fruits in summer.	○	Mid-spring	Height: 10–18' Spread: 15–20'	6 to 8	Full sun to full shade. Moist, well-drained, humus-rich soil. Cherry laurel withstands heavy pruning and can be shaped into a hedge. Scale insects can be a problem.
PTERIS BRAKE, STOVE FERN *Pteris cretica*	A small evergreen fern with broadly triangular fronds divided into pale green, fingerlike leaflets. Variegated cultivars are available.		No flowers	Height: 1–1½' Spread: 6–12"	9 to 10	Full sun to full shade. Moist, slightly acid, humus-rich soil. Brake doesn't grow well in soggy conditions. Plants can be grown indoors in containers in colder regions.
QUERCUS WHITE OAK *Quercus alba*	A stately tree with a broad crown. This eastern native has variable, 6-in.-long, round-lobed leaves that are dark green above and pale green below and turn brown in autumn. The light gray bark has flaky, blocky ridges when mature.	●	Mid-spring	Height: 50–80' Spread: 50–80'	3 to 9	Full sun. Deep, moist, well-drained soil that is slightly acid. This large tree is difficult to transplant and grows slowly. Transplant when small as a balled-and-burlapped tree.
RHODODEN-DRON FLAME AZALEA *Rhododendron calendulaceum*	A beautiful deciduous shrub native to the Southeast. Its clusters of 2-in., 5-petaled, funnel-shaped yellow, red, or orange flowers last several weeks. The 2- to 3-in.-long, glossy green leaves turn yellow, orange, or red in fall.	● ●	Late spring	Height: 4–8' Spread: 4–8'	5 to 8	Full sun (in the North) to full shade (in the South). Evenly moist, humus-rich, acid, well-drained soil. Mulch to maintain even moisture. Protect from drying winter winds. Avoid poorly drained and alkaline soils.

		Flower Color	Time of Bloom	Growth Habit	Hardiness Zones	Growing Conditions
	RHODODEN-DRON CATAWBA RHODODENDRON ◄ *Rhododendron catawbiense* 'Album' JAPANESE RHODODENDRON *R. mucronulatum*	*Shrubs with white or light purple, 1- to 2-in. flowers. Evergreen R. catawbiense has 3- to 6-in.-long, hand-some leaves that are dark above and light below. The 1- to 4-in. leaves of decid-uous R. mucronulatum are aromatic when bruised.*	○ ● R. catawb. Mid-spring to late spring R. mucron. Early spring	R. catawb. Height: 6–10' Spread: 5–8' R. mucron. Height: 4–6' Spread: 4–8'	R. catawb. 4 to 8 R. mucron. 4 to 7	*Full sun to partial shade. Evenly moist, well-drained, humus-rich, acid soil. Mulch to maintain even moisture. Protect from drying winter winds. Old leaves are shed in spring.*
	RHODODEN-DRON PINK-SHELL AZALEA *Rhododendron vaseyi*	*A deciduous azalea with medium green leaves that turn light red in autumn. The bell-shaped, 1½-in., bright pink, 5-petaled flowers are gathered in clusters of 5 to 8. A white-flowered variety is available.*	○ ● Mid-spring	Height: 5–10' Spread: 3–6'	4 to 8	*Full sun to partial shade. Evenly moist, well-drained, humus-rich, acid soil. Mulch to maintain even moisture. Protect from drying winter winds.*
	RHODODEN-DRON *Rhododendron yakusimanum*	*A small, dense, slow-growing rhododendron with thick, felted, evergreen leaves. The 10 or so flowers in a cluster are pink while in bud and change to white bells as they mature.*	○ Mid- to late spring	Height: 2–3' Spread: 2–3'	5 to 8	*Full sun to partial shade. Evenly moist, well-drained, humus-rich, acid soil. Mulch to maintain even moisture. Protect from drying winter winds. Old leaves are shed in spring.*
	RHODODEN-DRON DEXTER HYBRID RHODODENDRON *Rhododendron* hybrids	*Evergreen shrubs that are hybrids of R. fortunei and R. catawbiense and produce dense foliage and larger, more fragrant flowers than most rhododendron species. Flowers generally are lavender, white, or pink.*	○ ● ● Late spring	Height: 6–10' Spread: 5–8'	5 to 8	*Full sun (in the North) to partial shade (in the South). Evenly moist, well-drained, humus-rich, acid soil. Mulch to maintain even moisture. Protect from drying winter winds.*
	RHODODEN-DRON EXBURY HYBRID AZALEA, KNAP HILL AZALEA *Rhododendron* hybrids	*Deciduous shrubs with upright forms and leaves that turn yellow, orange, or red in autumn. There are many cultivars, with 2- to 3-in. clusters of trumpet-shaped white, pink, yellow, orange, or red unscented flowers.*	○ ● ● ● Late spring	Height: 4–8' Spread: 4–8'	5 to 7	*Full sun (in the North) to partial shade (in the South). Evenly moist, well-drained, humus-rich, acid soil. Mulch to maintain even moisture. Protect from drying winter winds.*

◄ *Indicates species shown*

Plants for American Shade Gardens

		Flower Color	Time of Bloom	Growth Habit	Hardiness Zones	Growing Conditions
RHODODEN-DRON INDICA HYBRID AZALEA, SOUTHERN INDIAN HYBRID AZALEA *Rhododendron* hybrids	Relatively tender evergreen shrubs with 2- to 3-in., funnel-shaped flowers in red, white, or lavender. They are often grown in green-houses in winter as potted plants. Cultivars are available in single- or double-flowered forms.	○ ● ●	Early to mid-spring	Height: 6–10' Spread: 8–10'	8 to 10	Full sun (in the North) to partial shade (in the South). Evenly moist, well-drained, humus-rich, acid soil. Mulch to maintain even moisture. Protect from drying winter winds.
RHODODEN-DRON KURUME AZALEA *Rhododendron obtusum* hybrids	Azalea hybrids with lustrous evergreen leaves. (Most azaleas are deciduous shrubs.) Some cultivars have reddish leaves in winter. The funnel-shaped, 1- to 1½-in. flowers are rose, pink, salmon, white, or coral.	○ ● ● ●	Mid-spring	Height: 3–6' Spread: 5–8'	7 to 9	Full sun (in the North) to partial shade (in the South). Evenly moist, well-drained, humus-rich, acid soil. Mulch to maintain even moisture. Protect from drying winter winds. Old leaves are shed in spring.
RHODODEN-DRON P.J.M. HYBRID *Rhododendron* hybrids	Among the hardiest of rhododendrons, P.J.M. hybrids have dark, evergreen foliage that deepens to purple in autumn and winter. The rounded shrubs produce 3- to 5-in. clusters of bright lavender-pink flowers.	●	Mid-spring	Height: 3–6' Spread: 3–6'	4 to 8	Full sun to partial shade in the North; partial shade in the South. Evenly moist, well-drained, humus-rich, acid soil. Mulch to maintain even moisture. Protect from drying winter winds. Old leaves are shed in spring.
RHODODEN-DRON ROBIN HILL HYBRID AZALEA *Rhododendron* hybrids	Evergreen azaleas with glossy, dark green leaves. The 3- to 4-in., open-faced flowers often have ruffled petals and come in many pastel colors. One of the latest-blooming azaleas.	○ ● ●	Late spring to early summer	Height: 2–4' Spread: 2–4'	5 to 9	Full sun to partial shade. Evenly moist, well-drained, humus-rich, acid soil. Mulch to maintain even moisture. Protect from drying winter winds. Old leaves are shed in spring.
RHODOTYPOS JETBEAD *Rhodotypos scandens*	A mounded, deciduous shrub with pairs of 2- to 4-in.-long, sharply toothed leaves. White, cup-shaped, 4-petaled flowers are borne singly at the ends of the twigs. The black, pea-sized fruits persist through the winter.	○	Summer	Height: 3–6' Spread: 4–9'	5 to 8	Full sun to full shade. Fertile, loamy soil. Plants adapt to a wide variety of soil conditions.

			Flower Color	Time of Bloom	Growth Habit	Hardiness Zones	Growing Conditions
	RODGERSIA *Rodgersia podophylla*	A clump-forming perennial with 5- to 10-in.-long leaves divided into 5 to 10 leaflets that turn from bright green in spring to coppery bronze in summer. Clusters of tiny, creamy white flowers are borne in large, plumed clusters above the foliage.	○	Summer	Height: 4–5' Spread: 2–3'	5 to 8	Full sun to full shade. Fertile, humus-rich, moist to wet soil. Protect from hot, dry winds. Rodgersia is an ideal plant for pondside or woodland naturalizing.
	SANGUINARIA BLOODROOT *Sanguinaria canadensis*	A perennial with flower stalks rising in spring from 4- to 8-in. round leaves with scalloped edges. Single, 8-petaled, 2- to 3-in. white flowers last about a week, then produce 2- to 4-in. green pods. Rootstocks contain red sap.	○	Early to mid-spring	Height: 6–15" Spread: 1–2'	3 to 8	Full sun to deep shade. Humus-rich, moist, well-drained soil; areas under deciduous trees and shrubs are ideal. Bloodroot will spread slowly, forming an attractive ground cover for most of the summer. Provide winter mulch in zones 3–4.
	SANGUISORBA CANADIAN BURNET *Sanguisorba canadensis*	A perennial with clumps of compound leaves having 10–15 oblong, toothed leaflets. Tall, erect shoots bear 6-in. spikes of tiny, white flowers in bottle-brush-like clusters.	○	Late summer	Height: 2–6' Spread: 1–2'	3 to 8	Full sun to light shade. Wet or moist, humus-rich soil. Sanguisorba is a good plant for swamps, marshes, and wet meadows.
	SARCOCOCCA SWEET BOX *Sarcococca hookerana var. humilis*	A mat-forming evergreen that becomes a shrubby ground cover with glossy, narrow, 1- to 2-in.-long leaves. Fragrant white flowers produce black, fleshy, berrylike fruits.	○	Late winter to early spring	Height: 1–3" Spread: 1–5'	6 to 9	Partial to full shade. A wide variety of soils. Sweet box is not difficult to grow if kept out of full sun and given sufficient moisture. It spreads slowly by rhizomes.
	SHORTIA OCONEE-BELLS *Shortia galacifolia*	An attractive evergreen ground cover rare in its native southeastern sites but not in gardens. Glossy, round, 3-in.-wide green leaves redden in winter. Each 5- to 8-in. shoot bears a 1-in., nodding, white, pink, or blue flower.	○ ◐ ●	Early spring	Height: 4–8" Spread: 6–12"	6 to 9	Light shade to full shade. Humus-rich, moist, well-drained, acid soil; sandy loam with added humus is ideal. Shortia needs constant moisture but will not tolerate soggy conditions. Propagate by division in spring.

◄ *Indicates species shown*

Plants for American Shade Gardens

		Flower Color	Time of Bloom	Growth Habit	Hardiness Zones	Growing Conditions
SKIMMIA *Skimmia japonica*	An evergreen, domed shrub whose 2½- to 5-in., oblong leaves cluster at the ends of twigs. Leaves are medium green above, yellow-green below. Female plants bear terminal clusters of small, fragrant white flowers that produce ⅓-in. red fruits.	○	Mid- to late spring	Height: 3–4' Spread: 3–4'	7 to 8	Partial to full shade. Moist, humus-rich, acid, well-drained soil. Purchase both male and female plants to guarantee fruit production.
SMILACINA FALSE SOLOMON'S-SEAL, SOLOMON'S-PLUMES *Smilacina racemosa*	A woodland native with a cluster of tiny, white, foamy flowers at the tip of each 3- to 6-in. arching stem. Clasping leaves tend to be purple at their points of attachment. Beautiful red berries appear in summer.	○	Mid-spring to early summer	Height: 1–3' Spread: 9–12"	3 to 9	Dappled sun to full shade, with some afternoon shade in warm climates. Well-drained, evenly moist, humus-rich soil. Smilacina will grow in full sun, but plants will be smaller. Mulch during winter in cooler climates.
SORBUS EUROPEAN MOUNTAIN ASH, ROWAN *Sorbus aucuparia*	A small tree with a rounded crown, grown for both its flat-topped clusters of ¼-in., red-orange fruits and its attractive foliage. The 6- to 8-in.-long compound leaves have 9–15 toothed leaflets and are light green below.	○	Mid- to late spring	Height: 20–40' Spread: 15–30'	3 to 6	Full sun to light shade. Well-drained, evenly moist, acid soil. Rowan does not grow well where soils are alkaline. It grows best where summers are cool. Canker and fire blight can be problems, especially if trees are stressed.
STYLO-PHORUM CELANDINE POPPY *Stylophorum diphyllum*	A perennial with bright yellow, 2-in., poppylike, 4-petaled flowers borne in clusters of 3 to 5 above attractive, gray-green, deeply lobed rosettes of leaves. The flowers produce light green, spiny, capsular fruits.		Early to late spring	Height: 1–2' Spread: 1–1½'	5 to 8	Filtered sun to full shade. Humus-rich, slightly alkaline, evenly moist soil. Plants are easy to cultivate and will self-sow, but not aggressively. Stylophorum is an ideal choice for woodland naturalizing.
STYRAX JAPANESE SNOWBELL *Styrax japonicus*	A small deciduous tree with graceful branches that bear fragrant, white, ¾-in., 5-lobed, bell-shaped flowers. The ½-in., gray, oval fruits mature in late summer and fall to the ground in autumn.	○	Late spring	Height: 20–30' Spread: 20–30'	5 to 8	Full sun to partial shade. Moist, well-drained, humus-rich, acid soil. Prune to desired shape in late winter.

		Flower Color	Time of Bloom	Growth Habit	Hardiness Zones	Growing Conditions
	SYMPHORI-CARPOS SNOWBERRY *Symphoricarpos albus*	A dense deciduous shrub with pairs of elliptical, 1- to 2-in., blue-green leaves. Clusters of ¼-in., bell-shaped, pink flowers at the ends of twigs produce ½-in., ivory white fruits that persist from autumn into winter.	○	Late spring	Height: 3–6' Spread: 3–6'	3 to 7	Full sun to full shade. A wide variety of soils, including clay and alkaline soil. Plants spread by suckers. Prune snowberry in early spring to encourage vigorous growth and abundant flowering. Anthracnose fungus can be a problem.
	TIARELLA FOAMFLOWER *Tiarella cordifolia*	An evergreen perennial ground cover forming mounds of fuzzy, heart-shaped, light green leaves with sharp lobes that turn coppery bronze in autumn and winter. Spikes of foamy, 5-petaled white flowers are held above the foliage.	○	Mid- to late spring	Height: 8–12" Spread: 9–15"	3 to 8	Full shade. Humus-rich, moist to wet soil. Foam-flower will not grow well in full sun, especially if the soil dries out. Slugs can be troublesome.
	TORENIA BLUEWINGS, WISHBONE FLOWER *Torenia fournieri*	An annual bearing unusual 5-petaled flowers with dark blue-purple wing markings at their flaring tips. The throat of the flower is light lavender with a yellow blotch on the lowest petal. Cultivars have white or rose pink flowers.	○ ○ ●	Midsummer to early autumn	Height: 6–12" Spread: 6–8"	Tender annual	Partial shade. Well-drained, moist, fertile soil. This fast-growing yet frost-sensitive annual should be started indoors in regions with short growing seasons. Transplant it outdoors after the soil has warmed and danger of frost has passed.
	TRADES-CANTIA SPIDERWORT *Tradescantia × andersoniana*	A hybrid of a native perennial bearing 3-petaled blue, white, lavender, or pink flowers that last less than a day. Dozens of buds in each cluster give spiderwort a long blooming season. It has robust, attractive, blue-green grasslike foliage.	○ ○ ○ ●	Late spring to midsummer	Height: 1–2' Spread: 1–1½'	3 to 9	Full sun to partial shade. Well-drained, moist soil rich in organic matter. Mulch during winter in cooler climates. Divide clumps every several years to keep them flowering vigorously.
	VIBURNUM BURKWOOD VIBURNUM *Viburnum × burkwoodii*	A deciduous shrub with showy clusters of small tubular flowers and pairs of dark green leaves that turn reddish in fall. The fragrant flowers are pink in bud and turn white at maturity. The berrylike fruits are dark red.	○	Mid-spring	Height: 8–10' Spread: 5–8'	3 to 8	Full sun to partial shade. Well-drained, moist, fertile soil; avoid waterlogged soil. Viburnums are prone to rotting and disease if drainage is inadequate.

◄ *Indicates species shown*

Plants for American Shade Gardens

		Flower Color	Time of Bloom	Growth Habit	Hardiness Zones	Growing Conditions
VIBURNUM KOREAN SPICE VIBURNUM *Viburnum carlesii*	A deciduous shrub whose pairs of velvety, dark green, 1- to 4-in., heart-shaped leaves have irregularly toothed edges. Fragrant flowers in 2- to 3-in. clusters are pink in bud but open to display tubular white petals.	○	Mid-spring	Height: 4–6' Spread: 4–6'	4 to 8	Full sun to partial shade. Well-drained, slightly acid, evenly moist soil. To reduce root rot, avoid soggy soils. Prune after flowering in early summer. Korean spice viburnum is a slow-growing shrub.
VIBURNUM DOUBLEFILE VIBURNUM *Viburnum plicatum* var. *tomentosum*	A deciduous shrub with horizontal branches and small, white tubular flowers in flat, lacy clusters. Flowers precede the midsummer appearance of black, berry-like fruits. Pairs of dark green leaves turn reddish purple in autumn.	○	Mid-spring	Height: 7–10' Spread: 9–12'	5 to 8	Full sun to partial shade. Well-drained, moist, fertile soil; avoid waterlogged soils. Viburnums are prone to rotting and disease if drainage is inadequate.
VINCA PERIWINKLE ◄ *Vinca major* 'Variegata' *V. minor*	Evergreen ground covers with thin, sprawling stems and pairs of glossy, leathery, dark green or variegated leaves. Lavender-blue, 5-petaled flowers grow singly above the mat of foliage and are 2 in. wide in V. major and ³⁄₄ in. wide in V. minor.	●	Mid-spring to early summer	Height: 4–6" Spread: 10–24"	4 to 8	Full sun to full shade with some afternoon shade in warm climates. Any type of soil except dry. V. major 'Variegata' is often grown as an annual in containers.
VIOLA CANADA VIOLET *Viola canadensis* SWEET VIOLET ◄ *V. odorata*	Perennials with attractive heart-shaped leaves and ¹⁄₂-in. purple or white flowers. The fragrant flowers of V. odorata rise on stalks above 2-in., downy leaves. V. canadensis has leafy flower stems. Foliage may be evergreen in warm regions.	○ ●	Spring to early summer	V. canad. Height: 8–16" Spread: 6–12" V. odor. Height: 4–12" Spread: 6–12"	V. canad. 3 to 8 V. odor. 5 to 9	Full to partial shade. Moist, humus-rich soil. Both violets creep slowly by rhizome growth or self-seeding. Under ideal conditions plants may become rampant. Mildew and slugs may be problems.
WOODWARDIA VIRGINIA CHAIN FERN *Woodwardia virginica*	A fern with long (2- to 4-ft.), purple-stemmed fronds that rise from thick, creeping rootstocks. The fronds are cut into 12 to 18 pairs of opposite leaflets, each further divided into narrow, tapering subleaflets.		No flowers	Height: 2–4' Spread: 2–4'	3 to 9	Filtered sun to full shade. Moist to wet, humus-rich, peaty soil. Woodwardia is easy to grow as long as the soil is kept constantly moist. This plant is ideal for bog gardens or damp woodland settings.

Plant Hardiness Zone Map

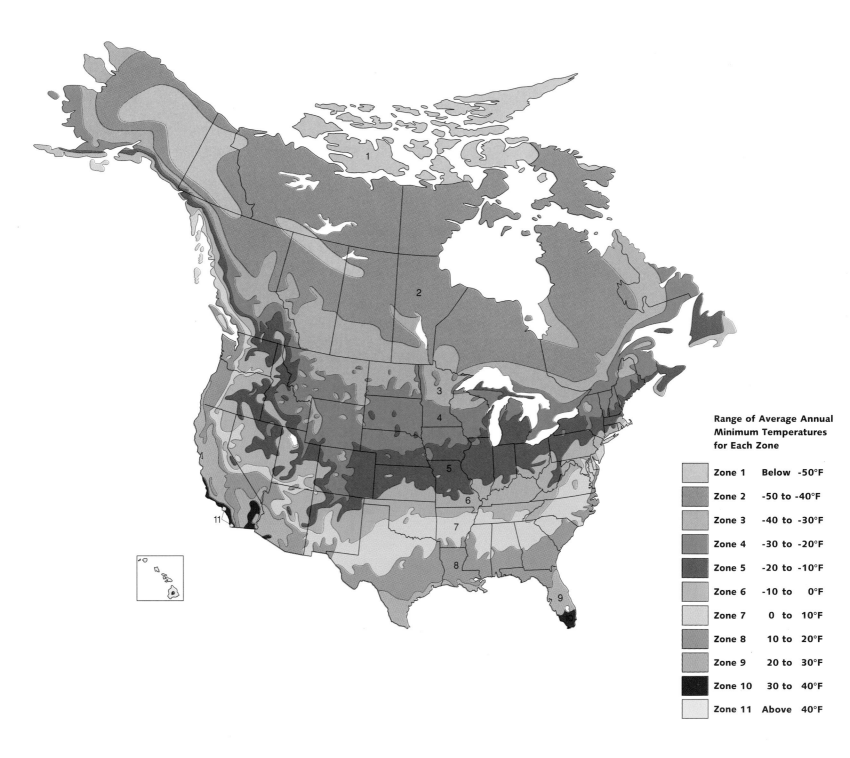

Range of Average Annual
Minimum Temperatures
for Each Zone

Zone 1	Below	-50°F
Zone 2	-50 to	-40°F
Zone 3	-40 to	-30°F
Zone 4	-30 to	-20°F
Zone 5	-20 to	-10°F
Zone 6	-10 to	0°F
Zone 7	0 to	10°F
Zone 8	10 to	20°F
Zone 9	20 to	30°F
Zone 10	30 to	40°F
Zone 11	Above	40°F

Resources for Shade Gardens

There are many dependable mail-order suppliers that can be helpful for landscaping with shade plants. A selection is included here. Most have catalogues available upon request (some charge a fee). An excellent source of further resources is Gardening by Mail by Barbara J. Barton. Updates on each edition are provided three times a year, available through subscription (forms provided in back of book); a new edition comes out every few years. To obtain this book, check your local bookstore or contact the publisher: Houghton Mifflin Co., 222 Berkeley Street, Boston, MA 02116. Telephone: (617) 351-5000.

Plants and Seeds

W. Atlee Burpee & Co.
300 Park Avenue
Warminster, PA 18974
215-674-4900
Large selection of perennials, trees, and shrubs for shady landscapes.

Kurt Bluemel, Inc.
2740 Greene Lane
Baldwin, MD 21013
410-557-7229
Specializes in perennials, ferns, aquatic plants, and ornamental grasses.

Bluestone Perennials
7211 Middle Ridge Road
Madison, OH 44057
800-852-5243
Perennials and selected shrubs, ornamental grasses, and ferns.

Carroll Gardens, Inc.
Box 310
444 East Main Street
Westminster, MD 21158
410-848-5422
Large selection of perennials, including many shade plants.

DeGiorgi Seeds & Goods
6011 'N' Street
Omaha, NE 68117-1634
800-858-2580
Plants and seeds, many for shady locations.

Holbrook Farm & Nursery
P.O. Box 368
115 Lance Road
Fletcher, NC 28732
704-891-7790
Specializes in perennials, native plants, and selected trees and shrubs.

Jackson & Perkins
P.O. Box 1028
Medford, OR 97501
800-292-4769
Known for roses, but also offers perennials, trees, and shrubs, as well as a collection of garden ornaments.

Klehm Nursery
197 Penny Road
South Barrington, IL 60010-9390
800-553-3715
Peonies, daylilies, hostas, grasses, ferns, and many other perennials.

Milaeger's Gardens
4838 Douglas Avenue
Racine, WI 53402-2498
800-669-9956
Over 300 varieties of perennials, including grasses and vines.

Park Seed Co.
Cokesbury Road
Greenwood, SC 29647
803-223-8555
Seeds, plants, bulbs, tools, and a wide selection of gardening supplies.

Shady Oaks Nursery
112 10th Avenue S.E.
Waseca, MN 56093
507-835-5033
Good selection of plants that grow well in shade, including hostas, wildflowers, and ferns.

Spring Hill Nurseries
6523 Galena Road
Peoria, IL 61632
513-667-2491
Plants and bulbs. Specializes in flowers, shrubs, ground covers, and houseplants.

Stokes Seeds, Inc.
737 Main Street
Louisiana, MO 63353
416-688-4300
Flower and vegetable seeds and supplies for commercial farmers and home gardeners.

Thompson & Morgan
P.O. Box 1308
Jackson, NJ 08527
908-363-2225
Seeds of all types and a wide range of garden supplies.

K. Van Bourgondien & Sons, Inc.
245 Farmingdale Road
P.O. Box 1000
Babylon, NY 11702-0598
800-552-9996
Specializes in bulbs, many suitable for shade.

André Viette Farm & Nursery
Route 1, Box 16
Fishersville, VA 22939
703-943-2315
Over 3,000 varieties of perennials for sun and shade.

Wayside Gardens
1 Garden Lane
Hodges, SC 29695
803-223-7333
Sophisticated ornamental plants, including many hard-to-find perennials.

White Flower Farm
Route 63
Litchfield, CT 06759
203-496-9624
Shrubs, perennials, supplies, books, and gifts.

Regional Specialties

Baycreek Gardens
P.O. Box 339
Grayson, GA 30221
404-339-1600
Many perennials suitable
for warm climates, including shade-tolerant species.

Busse Gardens
13579 10th Street N.W.
Cokato, MN 55321
612-286-2654
Wide selection of plants;
especially noted for cold-
hardy, rare perennials.

Corn Hill Nursery, Ltd.
R.R. 5
Petitcodiac, N.B.
Canada E0A 2H0
506-756-3635
Hardy stock for cooler
regions.

Hastings
P.O. Box 115535
Atlanta, GA 30310
404-321-6981
Large selection of flowers
and shrubs for southeast-
ern gardens.

High Altitude Gardens
P.O. Box 4619
Ketchum, ID 83340
208-788-4363
Seeds and plants that will
thrive in high altitudes and
arid conditions.

Ed Hume Seeds, Inc.
P.O. Box 1450
Kent, WA 98035
206-859-1110
Untreated flower, herb,
and vegetable seeds for
short-season climates.

Native Seeds/SEARCH
2509 N. Campbell #325
Tucson, AZ 85719
602-327-9123
Native seeds of the
Southwest and Mexico,
collected and propagated
with long-term preserva-
tion in mind.

Nichols Garden Nursery
1190 N. Pacific Highway
Albany, OR 97321
503-928-9280
Good selection of varieties
well suited for the
Northwest. Many fast-
maturing flowers and
herbs that warm-climate
gardeners can also use.

Porter & Son
P.O. Box 104
Stephenville, TX 76410
817-965-5600
Many older, hard-to-find
varieties. Also modern
hybrids that resist pests,
diseases, and hot weather.

Redwood City Seed Co.
P.O. Box 361
Redwood City, CA 94064
415-325-7333
Old varieties and a few
new ones, including many
unusual imports.

Supplies & Accessories

Alsto's Handy Helpers
P.O. Box 1267
Galesburg, IL 61401
800-447-0048
Classic garden furniture
and accessories, container
plants, and gift items.

Garden Way, Inc.
102nd Street & 9th
Avenue
Troy, NY 12179
518-235-6010
Mowers, rotary tillers,
garden carts, and other
lawn and garden
equipment.

Gardener's Eden
P.O. Box 7303
San Francisco, CA 94120
800-822-9600
Many items appropriate
for gardeners and some
ornamental shrubs and
outdoor containers.

Gardener's Supply Co.
128 Intervale Road
Burlington, VT 05401
800-955-3370
Useful gardening products,
including gifts, accessories,
greenhouse kits, and com-
posting equipment.

Kemp Company
160 Koser Road
Lititz, PA 17543
717-627-7979
Shredders, chippers, com-
posters, and supplies.

Mantis Manufacturing Co.
1458 County Line Road
Huntingdon Valley,
PA 19006
215-355-9700
Lawn and garden equip-
ment, including tillers,
chippers, and mowers.

The Plow & Hearth
301 Madison Road
Orange, VA 22960
800-866-6072
Outdoor furniture and
garden accessories.

Smith & Hawken
25 Corte Madera
Mill Valley, CA 94941
800-776-3336
Tools and garden supplies
as well as gardening hats,
shoes, and clothing.

Organic Gardening Products

Bio-Logic
418 Briar Lane
Chambersburg,
PA 17201
717-349-2789
Biological insect control
products, including
Scanmask.

Erth-Rite
RD1, Box 243
Gap, PA 17527
717-442-4171
Organic soil amendments,
Erth-Rite fertilizer, and
other soil enhancers.

Gardens Alive!
P.O. Box 149
Sunman, IN 47071
812-623-3800
Beneficial insects and a
complete line of supplies
for organic gardening.

Ringer Corporation
9959 Valley View Road
Eden Prairie, MN 55344
612-941-4180
Organic soil amendments,
beneficial insects, tools,
and irrigation equipment.

Safer, Inc.
60 William Street
Wellesley, MA 02181
617-964-0842
Pest controls, insecticidal
soaps, and natural and
botanical herbicides.

Index

Photo Credits